THE POLITICALLY COR

D0581261

The Politically Correct Phrasebook

What *they say* you can and cannot say
in the 1990s

NIGEL REES

BLOOMSBURY

First published 1993

This paperback edition published 1994
by Bloomsbury Publishing Limited
2 Soho Square, London W1V 5DE

The moral right of the author has been asserted.

Copyright © Nigel Rees 1993

A copy of the CIP entry for this book is available from the
British Library.

ISBN 0 7475 1427 5

Typeset by Hewer Text Composition Services, Edinburgh
Printed in Britain by Cox & Wyman Ltd, Reading, Berks

Contents

Introduction

The aim of this book is to illustrate the failure of communication that arises when everyday realities are dressed up in tasteful terms, thereby pandering to the squeamish and often obscuring the message. Much the same could be said of the terms 'politically correct' and 'political correctness' themselves. How did they acquire their present meanings – or, rather, the ones they had before they both became pejorative terms?

Originally, I suppose, a politician might have been said to make a politically correct decision when his electoral chances were not affected by it, never mind any questions of principle involved. Indeed, I came across such an example of the phrase in an old newspaper. With curious appropriateness, it is on the subject of votes for women:

> Mr Asquith's personal conviction on the subject is impenetrably unreasonable and atrociously insulting, besides being absurdly out of date in the face of the municipal franchise at home and the full franchise elsewhere; but as this is a free country for men, he has a right to his conviction. In acting on his conviction he is beyond reproach, consistent, fair, civil, personally pleasant under difficult circumstances and politically correct to the last degree. – *The Times*, 21 November 1911.

Much more recently, an American newspaper contains the phrase in (I take it) its original sense, but shading into the new:

> [Representative Barney Frank's] bill to repeal the two sections of the McCarran-Walter Act that exclude foreign visitors for their

political beliefs instead of their behaviour. The United States is the only Western democracy to impose such a test of political correctness, and Rep. Frank – among others – would like to dispose of it. – *The Washington Post*, 22 May 1984.

When did people in the United States start talking about political correctness in the current, specific sense? Appropriately enough, the first use of the phrase I have come across (though there may well have been earlier ones) dates, like the one just quoted, from 1984 (of all years):

What Langer has constructed is a facile evasion of the write-what-you-know doctrine. She is saying that novelists have a duty higher than the one they owe to their art and their private vision of the world; they have a duty to be politically correct... In thus construing, Langer reveals herself to be a captive of the assumption, widespread among the academic and literary left, that art exists to serve politics. – *The Washington Post*, 12 March 1984.

By the following year, the phrase in its modern sense is fully formed and stands alone without quotation marks:

It is the only caffeinated coffee served by the 'wait-persons', as they are called, at the politically correct Takoma Cafe in Takoma Park. – *The Washington Post*, 11 March 1985.

Other early citations include:

Now you can order Christmas gifts that are politically correct and simultaneously help Third World peasants and liberated American workers who are more interested in peace and justice than in mere money. – *The Washington Post*, 8 December 1986.

'The Oh So Politically Correct Players' are appearing regularly around town, aiming for laughs with their left-of-center political satire, songs and skits. – *The Washington Post*, 12 October 1987.

Then there are the 'Mr Feel Good' labels. These assure you a position in lefty heaven because you have bought ... politically-correct coffee beans made by workers in Nicaragua who will never use Hair Salad on contras. – *The Washington Post*, 27 December 1987.

[Wendy Chapkis] evolved, she tells us, from being a cute southern Californian blonde in the 1960s, to a radical San Francisco feminist in the 1970s. She adopted the sullen, but politically correct, insignia of 'the blue jeans, no make-up and hair-wherever-it-grew look'. – *The Sunday Times*, 27 March 1988.

A 'granola', taken from the nearest America has to muesli, is someone from the 1960s. Those people, though, are usually held by the new youth crowd to be 'PC'. This has nothing to do with [personal] computers. 'Politically correct' implies ideology aligned to the newly-emerging neo-left. – *The Times*, 24 December 1988.

Note that *The Times*, at this stage, is still introducing the concept to its readers in Britain.

The wrong word in the right place

Really, 'politically correct' and 'political correctness' are the wrong terms for the idea, in that they may make people think it has to do with Politics with a capital P, whereas it has much more to do with social concerns. Why not 'socially correct', then? – because that would make it sound as though it had something to do with manners and etiquette. 'Ideologically correct' would give the game away, of course, and leads us back to politics. As it is, 'political' hints at the coercion that is all too much part of the PC movement. In short, there cannot be a proper term for such a false concept. I amuse myself by sticking to the no-doubt-mistaken belief that 'politically correct' was formed on the basis of the phrase 'anatomically correct', a phrase that crops up in various medical contexts. For example, 'The Lippes loop [an intrauterine contraceptive device] is the next most anatomically correct, commercially available device' – H.J. Davis, *Intrauterine Devices for Contraception* (1971). But the term became more widely known when 'anatomically correct dolls' (i.e. dolls with genitalia) were used to enable children who might have been sexually abused to recount their experiences. They were much talked about in the UK during the Cleveland affair of 1987, when social workers claimed to have found child abuse in a large number of cases but were subsequently judged to have made wrong diagnoses.

Whatever the origins of the phrases, it is one of the purposes of this book to show that, although the notion of 'political correctness' and the term 'politically correct' both came to us from the United States at the beginning of the 1990s, the concept has long existed in other parts of the world. Awareness of racially pejorative terms stretches back many decades. Non-sexist usage, as promoted by feminists, has been with us since 1970, at least. Sensitivity regarding the nomenclature of the mentally and physically handicapped has also been the subject of earnest debate for many years. These have been issues of contention in Britain and elsewhere for as long as most of us can remember. It was merely that no name existed for the phenomenon.

Opponents of political correctness (PC) were, however, quick to invoke the terminology of the imagined excesses of totalitarianism as portrayed by George Orwell in his novel *Nineteen Eighty-Four* (1949). 'Newspeak' – the ambiguous, euphemistic language designed to meet ideological needs – is just like PC-speak. However, Newspeak's vocabulary is designed to shrink year by year, the ultimate object being to make heretical thought impossible, whereas politically correct language actually increases the vocabulary with its ever more verbose attempts at achieving the inoffensive phrase. 'Doublethink' – Orwell's term for the ability to hold two contradictory thoughts in one's mind at the same time – could also no doubt be found among the PC, if one bothered to look. Everyone has seen fit to liken the would-be enforcers of PC to the 'Thought Police' who ensured subservience to Big Brother in *Nineteen Eighty-Four*.

Again, there is nothing particularly new in the Orwellian name-calling of political and other euphemists, as the following citations show:

Accusing the Prime Minister of 'the same old excuses' it [*The Daily Telegraph*] labelled 'redeployment' as 'new-speak', which could be 'victimisation of the workers' in any but a Labour Government. – *Punch*, 27 July 1966.

The new party line, directed this time against 'rootless cosmopolitans' – newspeak for Jews. – *The Times Literary Supplement*, 11 August 1972.

Perfect bound ('newspeak' for 'unsewn') bindings on books have caused librarians grief and librarians money (for rebinding) since they fall apart so readily. – *Special Libraries*, 6 February 1977.

It is also not too far-fetched to relate the pursuit of political correctness to earlier attempts at achieving purity of language. In the seventeenth century, the French Academy began to weed out imports from other languages (even from Latin) – an attempt which has persisted even to our own day. In 1818, in Britain, Thomas Bowdler published *The Family Shakespeare*, a ten-volume edition of the dramatist's works with all the dirty bits left out (or, as he put it, 'those words are omitted which cannot be read aloud in a family'). 'Out damn'd spot' in *Macbeth* became 'Out crimson spot', and so on. Bowdler (1754–1825), in consequence, has given his name to any form of literary expurgation.

It is said, in fact, that Bowdler's sister Harriet was hotter on the subject than Thomas himself and that it was she who prepared the first *unsigned* edition. As she was a spinster, perhaps she felt it was wrong to show that she understood what she was expurgating. Whatever the case, one cannot help wondering whether the word 'bowdlerize' caught on because of its closeness to 'disembowel'. It was already current by 1836.

A rogue by any other name

The PC Police are professionals in the art of euphemism. By 'euphemism', we mean the saying of something in a gentler, more indirect way and one less likely to offend. I am inclined, therefore, to describe PC phrases as, for the most part, 'euphemisms with *attitude*' (in the current sense of that word), because they are not just softer, less offensive ways of saying things: they make, in addition, statements over and above their meanings. But in seeking to avoid giving offence of a racist, sexist, or other kind, to certain minorities, they often smell of calculation and compromise.

Worse, the word 'euphemism' is a word derived from the Greek *euphemos* meaning 'fair of speech' but most modern euphemistic coinages are not fair-sounding at all. What *The Oxford English Dictionary* (Second Edition) calls 'the substitution of comparatively favourable implication or less unpleasant associations, instead of the harsher or more offensive one that *would more precisely designate what is intended*' (my italics) more often than not leads to coinages that are contrived, clumsy and lacking the vigour of speech that has evolved through use rather than enforcement.

In fact, my chief objection to the political correctness movement and to politically correct phraseology, on grounds other than its frequent ludicrousness, is that through them direct, colourful words are invariably being replaced by dull, lifeless ones. PC words lack the true-life vividness of natural coinages. Invariably, also, by seeking to avoid some imagined offensiveness, words and phrases are produced that are less precise in their descriptiveness.

This process was in train long before PC was born. Apparently it was during the dark days of the Second World War that Westminster Council suddenly took it upon itself to start calling rat catchers, 'Rodent Officers'. Elsewhere, at about the same time, rat catchers also probably failed to recognize themselves as 'Rodent Operatives', as they came to be called. Why did officialdom make these changes? Was it because rat catchers had been complaining that their name made it difficult for them to make polite conversation when they were asked at dinner parties what they did for a living? I doubt it. While the bombs crashed around Westminster, I suspect that some bureaucrat sought to endear himself to what was quite clearly an oppressed minority by giving it a less meaningful name. But, after all, what does a 'Rodent Officer' or 'Operative' actually *do*? Does he nurse them, police them, or make them work? At least, when people said they were 'rat catchers' you knew precisely what they did.

Fifty years later, the same problem looms large in PC-dom. What is a 'physically different' person? We are all of us physically different from someone or something else and the expression gives not the slightest hint of what it is trying to say (in fact, that someone is physically *handicapped*). As for 'person of colour', the phrase may gain points for 'putting people first' (that is, putting the person before the fact that they have a distinctive colour), but it does not *define* whatever it is that is attempting to be said.

'Watch your language' may well be the slogan of the PC, and good advice that is, too, yet it is one thing to identify what is wrong with words and quite another to come up with substitutes that are not only more 'correct', in some sense, but are also as good as, or better than, what they replace. The politically correct may be quite correct in divining that something is the matter, but all too often they are incapable of doing anything sensible or effective about it. How often have people complained of a word like 'mastery' (because of its supposed sexist connotation) but been proved incapable of suggesting what they would rather put in its place?

Inappropriately directed laughter

While attempting to place political correctness in the broader context of earlier corrective euphemisms regarding race and of bureaucratic euphemisms dealing with menial jobs, and while recording some of the wilder effusions and jokes that surround the subject, this book has to tread a dangerous path. It may, for example, be accused of belittling the attempts to find appropriate expressions for the disabled by including them in a book devoted to political correctness and its accompanying sillinesses.

Unfortunately, however, the arguments that rage around the words and phrases used to describe the physically and mentally disabled are the same type of arguments that occur wherever political correctness is indulged in. The search for acceptable, positive expressions for the disabled is part of the phenomenon of euphemism in recent years with which this book is also concerned.

Think, for example, of the largely successful efforts made since the early 1960s to have the phrase 'Down's syndrome' substituted for 'mongolism'. A substantial body of opinion held that talk of 'mongolism' was racially offensive, quite apart from being upsetting for parents. The substitution cannot now be faulted on grounds of clarity, though I suspect most people using the term have no idea who 'Down' was. So this is included in the book to indicate how the search for the inoffensive term does not have to end in the woolliness of much PC coinage.

At the same time, there is no denying that a good deal of entertainment is to be had out of the whole PC fad. I don't happen to agree with those who believe that the phenomenon will soon collapse because the rest of the world is inclined to laugh it out of court. I believe that the urge to euphemism is so deep-seated that the devout will not easily let ridicule put them off their stroke. The matter is with us for a good while yet. But while it is with us, we may as well enjoy its absurdities.

You could say that a person who has difficulty with words is 'linguistically challenged' or you could say the same of someone who was rendered speechless by the idiocies perpetrated by PC. As far as I know, however, 'linguistically challenged' has never seriously been advanced as a PC phrase. It is but another invented example to add to many such thrown up by the British media since PC became known over here. 'Vertically challenged', meaning 'above or below average height', may well once have been an actual American example of PC. It is hard to tell. 'Aesthetically challenged' – meaning 'ugly' – is definitely a concoction.

This latter type is a humorous but positive reaction to what may once have been a well-meaning attempt to do the right thing with language but one which went hopelessly out of control. Laughter is the best response – if only because the PC Police are so dauntingly lacking in any trace of humour at all. Nevertheless, although it pains me to do so, I have felt it necessary to 'flag' the jokes in this book, to indicate where the serious stuff ends and the spoofery begins. A good deal of what is taken to be actual PC-speak is no more than inventive mockery by columnists and editorialists who, almost to a person, are agin it. A 1986 *Private Eye* story that a London borough had renamed its 'bottle bank' a 'bottle rehabilitation centre' (to avoid the utterly un-PC – and probably monetarist – term 'bank') turned out to be no more than an April Fool's Day joke. The price of pedantry is eternal vigilance.

An idea whose time had come

This book is not about the ideas of political correctness as such, simply its terminology, but the two things cannot be divorced from one another entirely. As should be apparent, the concept of political correctness was washing about during the 1980s on both sides of the Atlantic, even if it was not always called this by name. How then did it turn into a phenomenon?

The drives and attitudes behind political correctness became most noticeably established on the campuses of American universities amongst both students and teachers. It is said that the principal drivers were ageing radicals from the 1960s who were now in a position to make life difficult for academics perceived as being less than 'right on' in their attitudes towards feminism, ethnicity, and the problems of disadvantaged minorities of every conceivable kind.

There occurred certain well-publicized cases where academics were ousted on the grounds that they were against the spirit of the age. The American critic Harold Bloom, himself one who suffered, coined the term 'the School of Resentment' to describe those who applied PC techniques particularly to the teaching and study of literature. Students as well as academics became caught up in thought-policing which at times could be as vicious as the kind of thing practised by Red Guards waving their 'little red books' during the Chinese Cultural Revolution of the 1960s.

It was ideas and attitudes that were chiefly called into question but, running alongside, there was an extreme sensitivity over the language in which these were expressed. Hence, the manufacture of 'OK' terms and phrases that conformed to the positive '-isms' of the day.

Americans with their love of grandiose and verbose terminology were obviously well placed to take part in this process. The people who would always prefer to talk about 'homework' as 'an evening work study program', or who had given the term 'extra-vehicular activity' to what you did when you climbed out of your spacecraft, knew whereof they spoke. At the beginning of 1991, *Newsweek* ran a cover story (inevitably entitled 'Thought Police') and carried other material that firmly put the issue in the consciousness of the American public. By May 1991, word person William Safire in *The New York Times* was busy defining phrases like 'politically correct' and 'physically challenged' as, 'Adverbial premodified adjectival lexical units'. During the summer, political correctness was said to have 'swept through US universities'. In August, Joel Connaroe was writing, also in *The New York Times*: 'The phrase... has become a lethal weapon for silencing anyone whose ideas you don't like ... the McCarthyism of the left.'

This kind of charge became equally telling when, round about the same time, British journalists and columnists started writing horror stories on the subject. It was easy to use the phenomenon as an excuse for a spot of leftie-bashing, not to mention a touch of covert racism and masculinism. Most of the papers and magazines that reacted with such horror to the advance of political correctness were right-wing of view. But, on the other hand, to balance accusations that PC people were simply malcontents looking for something to do following the fall of communism, there were those who could remember the McCarthyism of the right, not to mention those in Britain who could identify the enforcing of conservative ideology (and speech) in what used to be known as the Establishment.

The reaction of pundits in Britain as well as America is important when considering political correctness as a phenomenon. The vigour and venom with which so many of them fell upon the topic has enabled some to charge that they blew it up − not to say invented the whole thing – as a way of bashing the left and indulging in other meaner prejudices. The distinction between the PC terms they invented for themselves (at which they then fell about in thigh-slapping merriment) and the real thing became confused. But, as I say, opponents of PC cannot claim victory. Political correctness won't be blown away that easily, though it may take other forms. No self-respecting PC policeman would now use the term 'politically correct', except in self-mockery (if such a thing were possible). The term has become the property of the enemy.

PC Person – advance and be recognized

It should be apparent by now that *The Politically Correct Phrasebook* does not take exactly what you would call a reverential approach to its subject. But let it not be forgotten that, however misguided PC persons may be, they are basically well-intentioned. Attempting to prune offensive, pejorative, racist (or whatever) terms from the language can hardly be considered an unworthy aim. The ways in which this is done, however, may be called into question. The point is that a very narrow line exists between euphemism that has a certain usefulness and euphemism that is no more than the pursuit of gentility for its own sake.

In examining the material for this book, I have been aware that all too frequently we only hear or read about PC people at second or third hand. Their supposed views are invariably filtered through the biased pens of their opponents. I have even found myself wondering at times whether they actually exist – these people hell-bent on the eradication of prejudice at all costs – so grotesque an image is conveyed of them by the media.

But, yes, PC enforcers do exist, even though they would never identify themselves as such nowadays. I have encountered them in broadcasting, in publishing (though chiefly in the US), in business and in local government. There is resentment and an absence of good humour in their attitude. An element of the busybody, too: how often it is that oppressed groups such as 'queers' and 'cripples' couldn't care a fig for what you call them – indeed, they may actively use the 'pejorative' names for themselves – while it is the professionally sensitive and the self-appointed carers who do all the offence-taking, supposedly on behalf of the oppressed.

The rest is herstory

Even before political correctness became an established phenomenon, it is probably true to say that even the most unreconstructed racist or uncaring male chauvinist had got the message that there were people who would rather they weren't that way. An awareness of the sensitivities of others – whether these be about sexist language or how you shouldn't refer to other races and nationalities – has become more general. Even if only wafer-thin, even if remembered only to be presented with self-mocking irony, certain advances have been made.

Another trouble with PC, however, is that it tends to encourage what is best described using the old phrase 'lip service'. The speaker who has been made aware of PC attitudes may say words that are ideologically sound, knowing that they are what is expected, but may still be thinking the wrong thoughts.

> When someone says 'Asian', they very seldom mean 'Asian'; they mean 'Indian' or 'Pakistani'. 'Ethnic' should be able to signify any cultural area, but when was the last time it was used to mean 'French' or 'Scottish'? When was the term 'the Asian community' used to refer to the Japanese in Britain? . . . That's the way that political correctness works. You say only the numbers, but you think of the sandwiches by name. – *The Independent*, 20 January 1992.

That puts the problem rather well. If this book has a purpose other than being a romp through the barmier purlieus of the English language, it may help to reveal the superficiality behind much self-proclaimed 'sensitivity'.

Acknowledgements

I am most grateful to Kathy Rooney and Tracey Smith of those most sensibly correct of publishers, Bloomsbury, for having invited me to put this phrasebook together. For once, I believe I have produced an impeccably non-sexist text and one without the need for an Author's Note on that subject. If one is felt necessary, may I refer the reader to the selection under DISCLAIMERS in the A-Z directory that follows.

My friend John M. Cone in Dallas, Texas, directed me to some rich American sources. Marlene Pease, producer of BBC Radio's magazine for disabled people, *Does He Take Sugar?*, provided me with its 'Guide to the Representation of People With Disabilities in Programmes' and other materials. Jon Naismith, producer of my programme *Quote ... Unquote*, lifted the veil for me on the BBC's 'Guidelines for Factual Programmes' with particular regard to the use of sexist expressions on the air. My wife, Sue, has shared with me her experiences on the wilder shores of feminism, in business, and in the field of psychotherapy. For published sources, please see the Bibliography at the end of the book and the source notes throughout.

How to Use This Book

The headwords of each entry are shown in bold print. Politically *correct* terms are shown in **bold** upper and lower case, e.g. **African-American**. Politically *incorrect* terms are set **bold** within square brackets, e.g. **[wop]**. Larger concepts, whether politically correct or incorrect, are listed in bold capitals, e.g. **WOMANISM**. Cross references are in SMALL CAPITALS.

The Politically Correct Phrasebook

A

abbess: See [-ESS SUFFIX].

-abled: This suffix means 'able bodied, and not DISABLED'. Usually preceded by an adverb – **differently abled, otherly abled, uniquely abled**, but also **otherwise abled** – these formations were introduced in the US at the beginning of the 1980s as a kinder, more positive way of regarding and describing disability.

Disabled, handicapped, differently-abled, physically or mentally challenged, women with disabilities – this is more than a mere discourse in semantics and a matter of personal preference. – Debra Connors, *With the Power of Each Breath* (1985).

In a valiant effort to find a kinder term than handicapped, the Democratic National Committee has coined differently abled. The committee itself shows signs of being differently abled in the use of English. – *The Los Angeles Times*, 9 April 1985.

Terms such as 'physically challenged', 'differently abled', and 'special' crop up occasionally, usually in an attempt to side-step the stigma of disability, but such phrases are not widely used nor much liked by disabled people generally. An accurate and un-patronising approach need not compromise plain language. There is little value in using words and phrases which tip-toe around the subject. – 'Guide to the Representation of People With Disabilities in Programmes', compiled by Geoffrey Prout (BBC, 1990).

[Quoting 'Definitions', Smith College Office of Student Affairs, 1990] . . . 'Differently abled' is a term created to underline the concept that differently abled individuals are just that, not less or inferior in any way . . .' Well, many people with handicaps surely do develop different abilities, but that is not what makes them a category. They lack something other people possess, and while that is not a reason to oppress them, it does violence to logic and language to pretend otherwise. – Jerry Ardler et al., 'Thought Police', *Newsweek*, 14 January 1991.

Compare -CHALLENGED and see also TEMPORALLY/TEMPORARILY-ABLE(D).

(*Sources include: The Oxford Dictionary of New Words*, 1991.)

ABLE-BODISM/ABLE-BODIEDISM: See next entry.

ABLEISM/ABLISM: Perceived discrimination in favour of able-bodied people and against the unfit and the DISABLED. The word was coined by US feminists in the early 1980s, but the notion has also been expressed (especially in the UK) through the words **ABLE-BODISM** and **ABLE-BODIEDISM**. Given that none of these words is easy to say, it is not surprising that the concept has hardly entered into mainstream usage.

A GLC report . . . referred throughout to a new phenomenon called mysteriously 'able-bodism' – a reference apparently to that malevolent majority, the fully-fit. *The Daily Telegraph*, 1 November 1984.

The Labour Party in Haringey has come up with the 'ism' to cap the lot. The latest term . . . is 'ableism', presumably coined to describe those sinners who discriminate in favour of able-bodied persons for jobs on building sites. – *The Daily Telegraph*, 8 November 1986.

Ableism – oppression of the differently abled, by the temporarily able. – 'Definitions', Smith College Office of Student Affairs (1990).

An example of how ableism may be unconscious:

> Even when journalists think that they are presenting positive images of disabled people, by praising them for achieving something that would be unremarkable if done by an able-bodied person, all too often this is patronising to disabled people, and reinforces stereotypes. – Briefing Note, The Royal Association for Disability and Rehabilitation, May 1992.

(*Sources include: The Longman Register of New Words,* 1989; *The Oxford Dictionary of New Words,* 1991.*)*

[abominable snowman]: See [SNOWMAN].

Aboriginal/Aborigine: Referring to the original, pre-colonial inhabitants of Australia, and their descendants, this is still the PC term. But how to refer to the majority of Australians – that is to say, **[white Australians]** and other **[immigrant Australians]**? The answer would appear to be **non-aboriginals**:

> Though [Bob] Hawke, the son of a congregational minister and nephew of a former Australian premier, will talk about the programme he instituted to have 'aboriginal Australians and non-aboriginal Australians' (political correctness has clearly crossed the last frontier) holding hands by the millenuium. – *The Sunday Times,* 22 March 1992.

-ABUSE: Misuse of any substance; maltreatment of another person – as in **alcohol abuse, child abuse, drug abuse, heroin abuse, ritual abuse, satanic abuse, solvent abuse, substance abuse.** So used in the first sense since the 1960s and in the second since the 1970s, but both constructions were especially prevalent in the 1980s. When applied with reference to drugs and other 'substances', it has always struck me as an odd construction. Although both alcohol and drugs can be used 'properly', the term 'substance abuse' suggests that the blame is placed on the substance rather than the user and also implies that the substance could never be used in a proper manner.

Pot-smoking is widespread in spite of dire warnings about the dangers of 'drug abuse' repeatedly broadcast by the armed forces radio. – *The Times*, 28 May 1970.

Child abuse occurs in all walks of life . . . Doctors and lawyers, too, batter their kids. – *The New York Times*, 6 January 1974.

This is a setback for the campaign against increasing heroin abuse among the young in all parts of the country. – *The Sunday Times*, 9 December 1984.

In the US, 'substance abuser' has now largely replaced 'drug addict' and **[drunk]**.

(*Sources include: The Oxford Dictionary of New Words*, 1991.)

accommodation: See RAILSPEAK.

[accompanist, piano]: Lest this term be taken to suggest that accompanists are in a subsidiary, submissive position, it should apparently be replaced by the PC **collaborative pianist**.

It was disheartening to learn from the programme-book that in America Miss Garrett is a 'leading teacher' of 'collaborative pianists' . . . Throttled submission is not collaboration. Must Americas have another generation of keyboard-doormats? – *The Economist*, 16 June 1992.

acquaintance rape: See DATE RAPE.

actor: Given that many **[actresses]** are active and vocal feminists, it is not surprising that they choose to call themselves 'actors'. This enables other people to rub them up the wrong way by sticking to the older usage:

It seems to be a rule of British intellectual life that the more distinguished the actress, the sillier her views – Vanessa Redgrave springs to mind, as do the trio of thespians who picketed Downing Street about pesticides in their babies' fruit juice. And perhaps no-one should worry too much about their political and cultural opinions. But actresses (and actors), being particularly sensitive to other people's ideas, are very good cultural weather vanes. – *The Sunday Telegraph*, 24 November 1991.

We actors are in the main regarded as licensed fools. Either that, or emotionally and intellectually retarded. – Glenda Jackson, quoted in *The Sunday Telegraph*, 26 July 1992.

However, it may be noted that the term 'actor' was apparently used for both sexes before the invention of 'actress' and, in any case, has been incorporated in the title of the Actors' Guild in the US and British Actors' Equity.

(*Sources include:* Rosalie Maggio, *The Nonsexist Word Finder: A Dictionary of Gender-Free Usage*, Boston, Mass., 1988.)

See also [-ESS SUFFIX].

[A.D.]: See C.E.

additive-free: See -FREE.

AIDS, person with: See [-VICTIM].

animal-free: See -FREE.

[adipose]: See [FAT].

[adulteress]: See [-ESS SUFFIX].

[adultery]: See CONSENSUAL NON-MONOGAMY.

adult male: The PC correct way of referring to a [MAN] – at least according to *The New York Times* style book (quoted in *The Independent*, 21 July 1992).

[adventuress]: See [-ESS SUFFIX].

aesthetically challenged: Rather than [UGLY]. See -CHALLENGED.

[afflicted by]: See under DISABLED.

African-American/Afro-American: In the United States, African-American is currently the almost mandatory replacement for 'black' or 'Black' – though not necessarily among blacks themselves. So it must be used with care, discernment and sense. There is a story told of a (white) American female TV reporter interviewing either Bishop Desmond Tutu or Nelson Mandela in South Africa. She was apparently so intent on avoiding the word 'black' that she asked the interviewee what it felt like being an 'African-American'.

It is not totally clear why African-American has emerged in preference to *Afro*-American at the present time. Both terms have been in use in North America (and elsewhere) since the mid-nineteenth century (there is even an 1835 example of the term **Africo-American**):

In our opinion, the true policy of the Afro-American race . . . is to emigrate to Canada, the West Indies. – *Voice of the Fugitive* (Windsor, Ontario), 21 June 1853.

She is a New Orleans Creole, her mother being an Afro-American, and her father a Louisiana Frenchman. – *Westminster Gazette*, 31 May 1898.

Many blacks . . . came to see it [the African-American Institute] as a 'honky' (white) conservative force. – *The Guardian*, 1 May 1971.

Upon spotting the Afro-American, the Ghanaians shouted out, 'Hey, Negro!' The other . . . retorted angrily, 'I'm a Black Man, not a Negro. Don't call me Negro.' – *Black World*, May 1973.

Although there is still apparently an Afro-American Studies Department at the City University, New York, the 'Afro-' version is definitely less common that it once was. Could this possibly be because the word 'Afro' has predominantly come to be associated with the bushy hairstyle of the 1960s?

See also [NIGGER] and PEOPLE OF COLO(U)R.

(Sources include: The Oxford English Dictionary, Second Edition.)

Afro-Caribbean: A description used by some people of West Indian stock (mostly in Britain) to emphasize their roots (compare AFRICAN-AMERICAN/AFRO-AMERICAN and CARIBBEAN-AMERICAN in the US). Apparently, this usage is resented by some actual Africans on the grounds that the West Indies nowadays have precious little to do with matters African.

> Anyone even suspected of sexism, racism, smoking or cultural imperialism (alleging that, say, Christmas is in some way 'better' than an indigenous Afro-Caribbean feast) is out, out, out. – *The Sunday Telegraph,* 29 December 1991.

> His [Home Office minister's] comments coincided with a report confirming that ethnic minorities – particularly Afro-Caribbeans – are less likely to benefit from schemes to keep offenders in prison. – *The Independent,* 16 September 1992.

AFROCENTRISM: In the US, the attempted replacement of the EUROCENTRIC or 'Western' view of culture and history, especially that taught in schools and universities, with one more attuned to the African-American point of view.

ageful: See [OLD].

AGEISM/AGISM: Discrimination and prejudice against people on the grounds of their age, directed especially at the middle-aged and the elderly, but also (technically) at the young. Most commonly, ageism is the oppression of the young and of the old by the age-group in the middle. The term was coined in 1969 by Dr Robert Butler, a specialist in geriatric medicine, of Washington DC:

> We shall soon have to consider a form of bigotry we now tend to overlook: age discrimination or age-ism, prejudice by one age group toward other age groups. – Dr Butler, quoted in *The Washington Post*, 7 March 1969.

> 'Like sexism and racism, ageism has had its day,' said Dr Alex Comfort, a world expert on ageing. Old people had to get moving and be bloody-minded to improve their lot. – *The Grimsby Evening Telegraph*, 27 May 1977.

> 'Agism' is a new word in the lexicon of fashionable evils. Like ... sexism and racism, it seeks to express an old evil in a new way – in this case prejudice in thought and deed against the old. – *The Times*, 2 August 1982.

> Agism is bad for men but worse for women. An older woman – unless she has made the top – is invisible. No longer desirable, she is expected to be even more deferential and servile. – *The Guardian*, 13 May 1986.

> Norah [Baroness] Phillips has died too soon for she was working on a Bill to outlaw ageism. She wanted to forbid advertisements for jobs which defined ages for applicants. She was especially angry to find that many European Community jobs were limited to applicants under 30. – *The Independent*, 17 August 1992.

(*Sources include*: *Longman Guardian New Words*, 1986; *The Oxford Dictionary of New Words*, 1991; *The Oxford English Dictionary, Second Edition.*)

AGEIST/AGIST: One who promotes the above. Spelt 'ageist', the term was used in *Private Eye* (17 May 1985). Another citation:

> Books which feature dotty old women or men are ageist and not acceptable, and the only witch books we will include ... are those

like *Aunt Fred Is a Witch* which is about a wonderful, very individualistic old woman reclaiming the word witch from the negative to the positive. – Women's co-operative publisher, quoted in *The Sunday Telegraph*, 16 September 1992.

airline steward/[stewardess]: See [-ESS SUFFIX] and FLIGHT ATTENDANT.

[airman/airwoman]: Politically correct persons use instead **aviator, flier,** or **pilot.**

alcohol abuse: See -ABUSE.

[alcoholic]: Although the most famous organization for combating alcoholism is still known, as it has been since its formation in 1935, as Alcoholics Anonymous, attempts have been made elsewhere, over the years, to soften the term. 'We don't speak of alcoholics: we call them **problem drinkers**' (from a BBC interview, September 1977). To refer to a **person with a drink problem** is obviously kinder than to talk about a **[drunk]**. Oddly or not, ALCOHOL ABUSE is less widely heard than other 'abuse' phrases.
See also -ABUSE.

[alderman]: The PC Person would use **public official** or **council member**.

alternative body image, person with an: See [FAT].

ALPHABETISM: Discrimination against people according to the position of their surnames in alphabetical order. The term was coined by Ian Stewart (who presumably suffered at the hands of it) in *The New Scientist*, 22 Oct 1987.
See also -ISM.

[Amazon]: There is apparently no acceptable PC term for this kind of tall, strong, athletic woman, named after the mythical warriors. 'Eliminate', suggests Val Dumond in *The Elements of Nonsexist Usage* (New York, 1990).

[ambassadress]: See [-ESS SUFFIX].

American Indian/Amerindian: See [RED INDIAN].

anatomically correct: See Introduction.

[anchorman]: For the person who introduces or chairs a radio or TV programme (mostly in US usage), the PC prefer **anchor** or **presenter**.

animal companion: This is the PC preferred term for **[pet]**, presumably because the older term is thought to be condescending to animals, if not outright ANIMALIST.

> A person who believes that men and women are more significant than the rabbit or mouse is liable to be accused of 'Speciesism'. Even the word 'pet' is now frowned upon. President Bush was recently publicly corrected for using it [instead of] 'animal companion'. – *The Daily Telegraph*, 26 June 1991.

> Imagine the shift a children's tale would have to undergo to rid itself of all offending elements. 'It's raining nonhuman animal companions,' said Wendy and Melissa's father'. – Beard & Cerf, *The Official Politically Correct Dictionary and Handbook*, 1992, quoted in *The Washington Post*, 8 June 1992.

Hence, also, **non-human animal companion** and **household non-human animal**.

ANIMAL-FREE: See -FREE.

ANIMALISM: (1) Discrimination against animals, largely on the grounds that they are inferior to humans. (Compare SPECISM/SPECIESISM.) (2) Oddly enough, the complete opposite – the support and promotion of animals, on the grounds that humans are not superior to them.

Animalism (1) may also be detected in language used to describe humans. To call someone a **[bitch]** or even a **[silly ass]** constitutes a massive slur against two very fine types of animal (especially those represented by able lawyers).

Hence:

ANIMALIST: (1) One who supports animal rights and wishes to extend certain human rights to animals, an **animal liberationist**; (2) someone who is *against* animals. (Other meanings include: a follower of the philosophy of animalism and a painter of animal pictures.) Also used adjectivally.

The uproar resulted from a column two weeks ago in which I reported that animalist Barbara Toth was enraged over the possibility that some Asian immigrants in Canoga Park might be turning strays into dog foo young. – *The Los Angeles Times*, 22 July 1985.

Animal rights campaigners on Merseyside are urging parents and teachers to stop children using 'animalist' expressions, which they claim demean certain creatures. – *The Daily Telegraph*, 27 October 1989.

(*Sources include: The Oxford Dictionary of New Words*, 1991.)

ANIMAL LOOKISM: Showing a preference towards pretty animals such as butterflies over ugly ones such as slugs. Mentioned in *The Times* (30 June 1992), but known in the US since at least 1989.

anti-oppressive practices: What PC Persons commit themselves to in order to rid the world of OPPRESSIVE ATTITUDES.

Asian-American: This expression, used to describe an American of Asian descent, is preferred to **[Oriental]** on the grounds that the older word was not chosen by the oppressed people themselves but by 'other' people, namely, Europeans.

[David Henry Hwang] grins suddenly, and the smile lights up his face like a schoolboy. 'I remember my first play, FOB (standing for Fresh Off the Boat, about recently arrived Chinese immigrants to America) was staged at the Asian-American house at Stanford and then afterwards I had to have a 'self-criticism', a session so that the community could comment on the work.' – *The Times*, 17 March 1989.

Can we be sure, however, that Asian-Americans themselves chose to be described in this manner? What should Orientals who are not in the United States be called? Would they settle for Asian?

(*Sources include:* 'Definitions', Smith College Office of Student Affairs, 1990.)

[ass, silly]: See ANIMALISM.

aurally challenged: [DEAF]; HARD OF HEARING. See -CHALLENGED.

aurally inconvenienced: Preferred to [DEAF] or HARD OF HEARING. See also -CHALLENGED.

author/[authoress]: See [-ESS SUFFIX]

autoeuthanasia: See [SUICIDE].

aviator: See [AIRMAN/AIRWOMAN].

[aviatrix]: See [-RIX SUFFIX].

awareness exercises: What PC Persons do to winkle out OPPRESSIVE ATTITUDES in themselves and, chiefly, others.

B

[bachelor girl, bachelorette]: Use **single woman, unmarried woman**.

[backward]: See [MENTALLY HANDICAPPED].

[bag lady/baglady]: I feel this must be a politically incorrect term, though I had not encountered anyone who said it was until I read Rosalie Maggio's *The Nonsexist Word Finder: A Dictionary of Gender-Free Usage*, Boston, Mass., (1988). She says, 'The gender-fair use of "bag woman" and "bag man" (avoid the nonparallel lady/man) is sometimes appropriate, although we tend to hear a great deal more about the bag woman than we do about the bag man, even though statistically more men than women are forced into this lifestyle.'

Meaning, 'a female **[vagrant]**' and of US origin, the term 'baglady' refers to the vagrant's habit of carrying all her possessions about in the plastic bags supplied by supermarkets. The term has been part of American English since the 1970s and was in British English by 1986, usually as a pejorative term to describe any woman who looked a mess. Could there be a PC term for such a person? Well, **street person** has been suggested.

Variations include **[shopping-bag lady]** and, inevitably, **[bagperson]** – though this points up the fact that the trait is usually remarked on in female vagrants these days and is thus doubly non-PC. The term **[bagman]** has been used in Australian English to denote a (usually male) tramp who carries possessions in a bag, since the late 1890s. Compare [TRAMP].

(*Sources include: Longman Guardian New Words*, 1986.)

[bald/balding]: Any number of euphemisms have been found over the years for this condition – 'thin on top', 'thinning', 'with receding hair', 'with hair loss', 'with hairfall' – but while none is non-PC, none is actually very PC, either.

> Women get so obsessive about their hairfall that they often get the problem quite out of perspective. – *The Observer*, 9 October 1977.

PC euphemisms include **hair disadvantaged, differently hirsute**. See also FOLLICULARLY CHALLENGED and TRICHOLOGICALLY CHALLENGED under -CHALLENGED.

(*Sources include:* Vernon Noble, *Speak Softly – Euphemisms and Such*, 1982.)

[barmaid]: Among the attempts at upgrading this job description – and completely unsuccessful at that – have been 'bar assistant', 'bar attendant' and 'stewardess'. Writing of his mother's job when he was a boy in the 1930s, the playwright John Osborne quotes her as saying: '*I'm* not a barmaid. I'm a victualler's assistant – *if* you please.' (*A Better Class of Person*, 1981).

(*Source:* Vernon Noble, *Speak Softly – Euphemisms and Such*, 1982.)

[barren]: The correct terms for such a woman are **infertile** and **sterile**, not least because they can refer to both men and women. 'Avoid "barren" which carries a certain unwarranted stigma and is used only of women,' says Rosalie Maggio in *The Nonsexist Word Finder: A Dictionary of Gender-Free Usage*, Boston, Mass., (1988). 'Saying that someone is "childless" or "has no children" is not recommended as these phrases tend to support a child-as-norm stereotype.'

The condition was also described in *The Times* (5 May 1976) as being a **[sub-fertility problem]** – but this is plainly non-PC because of the non-positive word 'problem'.

(*Sources include:* Vernon Noble, *Speak Softly – Euphemisms and Such*, 1982.)

[bastard]: See -CHALLENGED.

B.C.E.: An abbreviation to be used in dating instead of **[B.C.]** (Before Christ). The initials stand for 'Before the Common Era' – a rather vague coinage which has, however, appealed principally to Jewish people because the unacceptable Christian element has been removed.

A glance at the Babylonian captivity (587-536 B.C.E.) – K. Magnus, *About the Jews* (1881).

Compare C.E.

bent: See GAY.

big: See [FAT].

[birth control]: See FAMILY PLANNING.

birth name: See [MAIDEN NAME].

[bitch]: See ANIMALISM.

black: See AFRICAN-AMERICAN, [NIGGER], and PEOPLE OF COLO(U)R.

[black coffee]: See [WHITE COFFEE].

[blind]: American suggestions include **unseeing person** and **visually impaired individual. Optically challenged** is more for **people with seeing difficulties** rather than those who are out and out blind. See -CHALLENGED.

[blonde]: American insistence is on **blond** for hair orientation of this type in both sexes. Also **brunet** for **[brunette].**

Leah Gardner watches as the bus doors open and a blond figure jumps out, dashes up the walk, and hurls herself into the kitchen. – Claudia L. Jewett, *Adopting the Older Child*, Boston, Mass., 1978.

See also ESSEX GIRL JOKES.

body harassment: Of one's own body, that is – what used to be called 'self-indulgence'. Compare the term 'sexual harassment' (current in the US by 1975).

> Both Churchills belonged to their age, but not to ours. Not far behind racism and sexual harassment on the charge sheet of politicial correctness comes 'body harassment' . . . The sins against the Holy Ghost of PC are smoking, drinking too much (or indeed at all), eating too much (or any cholesterol) and, as a recent addition, engaging in unsafe sex. – *The Daily Telegraph* (14 July 1992.

[bonny]: See [FAT].

[boring]: See DIFFERENTLY INTERESTING.

[broad in the beam]: See [FAT].

[bridesmaid]: American insistence is on **bride's attendant**.

brunet/[brunette]: See [BLONDE].

[broke]: See -CHALLENGED.

[burglar]: See OFFENDER.

[businessmen]: Remember that there may be 'businesswomen' as well. Use 'executive' when suitable.

(*Source:* 'Guidelines for Factual Programmes', BBC, 1989.)

[busmen]: Use instead, 'Bus drivers, conductors, bus crews, London Transport/Greater Manchester Transport staff'.

(*Source:* 'Guidelines for Factual Programmes', BBC, 1989.)

[butcher]: Early attempts at upgrading this term included making use of the phrase **family butcher** (to lessen, it was hoped, any

lingering association with the slaughterhouse) and **meat purveyor**
(which I don't believe ever caught on except in advertising painted
on the side of vans or on customized shopping bags).

(*Source:* Vernon Noble, *Speak Softly – Euphemisms and Such*, 1982.)

[buxom]: See [FAT].

C

Caribbean-American: An American of Caribbean descent who chooses rather to emphasize this rather than any AFRICAN-AMERICAN roots beyond that.

caring: What is done by carers – a term stretched almost to breaking point during the 1980s to include almost anybody concerned with social and welfare services. To my mind, it smacks of image-building and is not without a cringe element. Marginally worse is the facile rhyme of 'caring and sharing' which first grated on my ears when I heard it used repeatedly to promote a Telethon-type fund-raiser in Melbourne, Australia (November 1981).

> The love I feel for our adopted children is in no way less strong than the love I feel for the three children in our family who were born to us ... It is the caring and sharing that count. – Claudia L. Jewett, *Adopting the Older Child*, Boston, Mass., 1978.

> The teenagers on *Beverly Hills 90210* do not reject their parents' affluence ... They simply aspire to a version of it that is gentler, and more politically correct. Bobbed noses and BMWs, they reckon are not incompatible with a bit of superficial caring and sharing. – *The Economist*, 28 March 1992.

C.E.: Abbreviation for 'Common Era' – originally and still an almost exclusively Jewish usage designed to remove the Christian element from dating, as in **[A.D.]** meaning *'Anno Domini'* – 'in the year of Our Lord'. However, it has sometimes been taken to mean 'Christian Era', which surely defeats the object of the exercise.

Outlines of Jewish History from B.C. 586 to C.E. 1885. – Title of book by K. Magnus (1886).

Compare B.C.E.

[cell, police]: See CUSTODY SUITE.

cerebrally challenged: See -CHALLENGED.

cerebral palsy: Preferred term to describe what a **[spastic]** has.

Some diseases and disabilities are regarded by the general population with particular dread, so that the terms used to describe them have become stigmatizing and insulting and should always be avoided. Do not use spastic or mongol, instead refer to people as having cerebral palsy or down's syndrome. – Briefing note, The Royal Association for Disability and Rehabilitation, May 1992.

As with Mencap (see [MENTALLY HANDICAPPED]), the Spastics Society has been caught in the cross fire over PC nomenclature while working under a questionable banner. While apparently not wishing to interfere with an established name in order to suit current fashion, the Society does encourage references to 'people with cerebral palsy' rather than 'spastics'.

Spasticity relates to conditions which involve muscle spasms. Slang use of the word 'spastic' in a derogatory sense, meaning 'uncoordinated' or just plain 'stupid', draws forth from an editor of *The Oxford English Dictionary* (Second Edition), a rare initialled note: 'Although current for some fifteen years or more, it is generally condemned as a tasteless expression, and is not common in print – R.W.B[urchfield].'

cerebro-genitally challenged: See -CHALLENGED.

chair: The non-sexist term for a chairman or chairwoman was introduced by 1976 and has had a mixed reception, though it has demonstrated rather more staying power than one might have expected. As *The Oxford Dictionary of New Words* points out, reference to the 'chair' in this context is of long-established usage. **Chairperson** (which may actually have been introduced *before* 'chair') has never really caught on, except in a consciously mocking way, though it sometimes surfaces.

As with the invention of MS., the attempt at removing gender, in this case from 'chairman', has resulted in an oddity. Addressing someone as 'chair' is still faintly ludicrous. Declared Baroness Sear in 1988: 'I can't bear being called Chair. Whatever I am, I am not a piece of furniture.' Moreover, it is based on the mistaken premise that the 'man' in 'chairman' denotes masculinity. On the contrary, it merely reflects membership of the human race. Of course, this is what feminists object to in the first place: 'man' does, after all, contain the notion of masculinity. See [MAN].

'Madam Chairman' would seem to be an acceptable compromise. It is a touch pompous and formal but, given the context, that shouldn't really bother anyone.

A group of women psychologists thanked the board for using the word 'chairperson' rather than 'chairman'. – *Science News*, 11 September 1971.

She has annoyed the Black Sections by refusing to resign as chair of the party black advisory committee. – *Tribune*, 12 September 1986.

To detractors from the film and TV camps who demand to know why women need their own industry organization at all, Women in Film chairperson Brenda Reid has only one answer: 'You see, the boys already have their own organisation. It's called the British Film Industry.' – *The Guardian*, 12 December 1991.

Another method of dealing with the matter is provided in 'Guidelines for Factual Programmes' (BBC, 1989): 'One of the most difficult. Best to overcome the problem by turning the sentence round: Jane Smith, who chairs the council's policy committee.' The Guide also adds: 'Chairperson is acceptable if it does not needlessly arrest attention' – some qualification.

(*Sources include: The Oxford Dictionary of New Words*, 1991; Nigel Rees, *Best Behaviour*, 1992.)

-CHALLENGED: A suffix designed to convey a personal problem or disadvantage in a more positive light. Originating in the US, the first such coinage would appear to have been 'physically challenged' in the DISABLED sense.

> This bestselling author [Richard Simmons] of *The Never Say Diet Book* creates a comprehensive fitness program for the physically challenged. – *Publishers Weekly* (US), 10 January 1986.

Actual PC '-challenged' coinages are now far out-numbered by jocular inventions. Among the many suggested in Britain and the US have been:

aesthetically challenged	= ugly
aurally challenged	= deaf, hard of hearing
cerebrally challenged	= stupid
cerebro-genitally challenged	= being a dickhead
chronologically challenged	= old
constitutionally challenged	= under a dictatorship
ethnically challenged	= Jewish
financially challenged	= broke
follicularly challenged	= bald
gynaecologically challenged	= menstruating
horizontally challenged	= fat
humorously challenged	= unfunny
hygienically challenged	= dirty
ideologically challenged	= a political 'don't know'
intellectually challenged	= stupid
linguistically challenged	= dumb, speechless, with speaking difficulties, unable to speak foreign languages

metabolically challenged	= dead
morally challenged	= criminal
optically challenged	= partly sighted or blind
orthographically challenged	= unable to spell
paternally and socially challenged	= illegitimate
trichologically challenged	= bald
university challenged	= attending a polytechnic
verbally challenged	= with speech impediment
vertically challenged	= small, dwarf; smaller or taller than average
visually challenged	= ugly; partly sighted or blind

See also main entries on HYGIENICALLY CHALLENGED and ORTHO-GRAPHICALLY CHALLENGED.

(*Sources: The Washington Post*, 4 August 1991; Beard & Cerf, *The Official Politically Correct Dictionary and Handbook*, 1992; *The Independent*, 25 & 30 June, 1992; *The Times*, 28 June 1992.)

[chambermaid]: According to Val Dumond in *The Elements of Nonsexist Usage* (New York, 1990), the appropriate terms are **housekeeper**, **personal attendant**, and even **servant**.

CHAMPAGNE SOCIALISM: A very un-PC concept. It is obviously quite inappropriate for socialists to smile and have fun when the world needs putting to rights. Worst of all are those conspicuous consumers of fine wines and good food who nevertheless profess to be socialists – Raymond Postgate, founder of *The Good Food Guide* was an early example of this breed.

Currently, the most obvious example of a **champagne socialist** is John Mortimer, the prolific playwright, novelist and lawyer. Indeed, the phrase might seem to have been coined with him in mind – he does indeed like a bottle or two, goes around calling everyone 'darling', and doesn't see why the good things in life should be denied him just because he is a 'bit Left'.

[On the set of his latest television serial *Titmuss Regained*] Mortimer relaxed in the catering bus with a bottle of Moet (apparently determined not to disappoint those who think of him as a champagne socialist). – *The Independent*, 2 September 1991.

Embarrassingly, however, the earliest use of the term I have come across is in connection with that other larger-than-life character, the late and unlamented Robert Maxwell.

Robert Maxwell, *Daily Mirror* newspaper tycoon and possibly the best known Czech in Britain after Ivan Lendl, has long been renowned for his champagne socialist beliefs. – *The Times*, 2 July 1987.

I suspect that, almost certainly, the term has also been applied to Derek Hatton, the former deputy leader of Liverpool City Council.

After this, it is some comfort to find a similarly alliterative phrase being applied much earlier to an altogether more admirable larger-than-life socialist, Aneurin Bevan. Randolph Churchill (who was, of course, a champagne *Conservative*) recalled how Brendan Bracken had once gone for Bevan:

'You Bollinger Bolshevik, you ritzy Robespierre, you lounge-lizard Lenin,' he roared at Bevan one night, gesturing, as he went on, somewhat in the manner of a domesticated orang-utang. 'Look at you, swilling Max [Beaverbrook]'s champagne and calling yourself a socialist.' – *The Evening Standard*, 8 August 1958.

charm-free: Boring; unpleasant. See also DIFFERENTLY INTERESTING.

(*Source:* Beard & Cerf, *The Official Politically Correct Dictionary and Handbook*, 1992.)

[charwoman]: The suggested US term is **charworker** (or **janitor**). In the UK, another unacceptable term would be **[charlady]**. See under also CLEANING LADY.

Chicana/Chicano: By some, the preferred term for **Mexican-American**, and in use by the late 1940s. 'Chicana' is female, 'Chicano' is male – 'use gender-fairly', advises Rosalie Maggio in *The Nonsexist Word Finder: A Dictionary of Gender-Free Usage*, Boston, Mass., (1988).

child abuse: See -ABUSE.

childfree: Used by a writer in *The Listener* to describe childlessness *by choice* and described by another correspondent as 'an exceedingly nasty neologism' (3 March 1977). It had presumably been coined to avoid use of the negative **[childless].**

(*Source:* Vernon Noble, *Speak Softly – Euphemisms and Such*, 1982.)

[Chinaman]: The preferred term is **Chinese person** or, simply, **Chinese**, as in, 'He/she is a Chinese'. 'The offensive term "Chinaman" is racist as well as sexist,' says Rosalie Maggio, in *The Nonsexist Word Finder: A Dictionary of Gender-Free Usage*, Boston, Mass., (1988). 'Use "Chinese" for both men and women.'

    [Chink] – the offensive slang term, known by the early 1900s – is naturally right out.

[Christian name]: Use **first name**. In 1967, I was present when a TV producer asked Dr Goldberg, the Chief Rabbi of Manchester, what his Christian name was. To his credit, Dr Goldberg replied with a smile, 'My Christian name is Selwyn.'

[Christmas]: See KWANZAA.

chronologically challenged/gifted: See -CHALLENGED and [OLD].

CLASSIST: One who discriminates or is prejudiced against another person on grounds of social status, i.e. one who indulges in class prejudice. The concept of **CLASSISM** goes back to the mid-nineteenth century.

The sex, race, social station and general circumstances of a criminal are normally held to come into this category. I disagree. Any information about anybody is bound to be sexist, racist, classist, ageist or something. – *Private Eye*, 17 May 1985.

The user called another participant in the conversation 'a classist' for arguing that (particular) middle class values and behaviors were superior. – *American Speech*, Summer 1988.

[cleaning lady]: This term has gone the way of CHAIRWOMAN as have all the other traditional and affectionate ones: [Mrs Mopp], [my treasure], [my woman what does], [Mrs ... who comes in] and [my daily]. The term is now **cleaner** – and no possessive 'my', please – though **domestic/household help** is probably in order. **Domestic assistant** has also been known. An **office cleaning operative** would probably fail to recognize herself or himself.

(*Sources include:* Vernon Noble, *Speak Softly – Euphemisms and Such*, 1982.)

client: See [PATIENTS].

[coach]: See RAILSPEAK.

coffee with/without milk: See [WHITE COFFEE].

collaborative pianist: See [ACCOMPANIST, PIANO].

colonization: See [DISCOVERY].

[coloured]: See [NIGGER] and PEOPLE OF COLO(U)R.

companion: A curiously neutral and virtually nondescript term to describe any person or any pet, though it has been used to describe a homosexual lover. See also ANIMAL COMPANION.

company representative: See [SPOKESMAN].

[confined to a wheelchair]: See WHEELCHAIR-USER.

consensual non-monogamy: Term for [adultery] or [swapping sex partners]. A joke coinage from *The New York Times*, 22 March 1991.

constitutionally challenged: See -CHALLENGED.

consumer: See HOMEMAKER.

[contraception]: See FAMILY PLANNING.

[corrupt]: See ETHICALLY DIFFERENT.

cosmetically different: For [ugly]. See also -CHALLENGED.

(*Source:* Beard & Cerf, *The Official Politically Correct Dictionary and Handbook,* 1992.)

council member: See [ALDERMAN].

counter-factual proposition: A term for [lie] – a joke coinage from *The New York Times*, 22 March 1991 – though probably more to do with the art of bureaucratic euphemism than with mainstream PC.

This recalls two earlier bureaucratic euphemisms for the same word. The status of Chinese workers in South Africa was mentioned in the King's speech to Parliament in 1906 as 'slavery'. Hence, an Opposition amendment of 22 February of the same year regretting, 'That Your Majesty's ministers should have brought the reputation of this country into contempt by describing the employment of Chinese indentured labour as slavery.' Winston Churchill, as Under-Secretary at the Colonial Office, replied by quoting what he had said in the previous election campaign:

The conditions of the Transvaal ordinance under which Chinese Labour is now being carried on do not, in my opinion, constitute a state of slavery. A labour contract into which men enter voluntarily for a limited and for a brief period, under which they are paid wages which they consider adequate, under which they are not bought or sold and from which they can obtain relief on payment of seventeen pounds ten shillings, but it cannot in the opinion of His Majesty's Government be classified as slavery in the extreme acceptance of the word without some risk of **terminological inexactitude.**

This phrase has been taken, almost invariably, as a humorously long-winded way of saying 'lie', but the context shows that this is not the meaning. One of the first to misunderstand it, however, was Joseph Chamberlain. Of 'terminological inexactitude' he said: 'Eleven syllables, many of them of Latin or Greek derivation, when one good English word, a Saxon word or a single syllable, would do!'

On 18 November 1986, the British Cabinet Secretary, Sir Robert Armstrong, was being cross-examined in the Supreme Court of New South Wales. The British Government was attempting to prevent publication in Australia of a book about MI5, the British secret service. Defence counsel Malcolm Turnbull asked Sir Robert about the contents of a letter he had written which had been intended to convey a misleading impression. 'What's a "misleading impression"?' inquired Turnbull. 'A sort of bent untruth?'

Sir Robert replied: 'It is perhaps being **economical with the truth.**' This explanation was greeted with derision not only in the court but in the world beyond, and it looked as though a new euphemism for lying had been coined. In fact Sir Robert had prefaced his remark with, 'As one person said . . .' and, when the court apparently found cause for laughter in what he had said, added: 'It is not very original, I'm afraid.' Indeed not, earlier users of the idea had included Sir William Strang (1942), Arnold Bennett (1915), Mark Twain (1897), Edmund Burke (1796) and Samuel Pepys (1669/70).

(*Sources include:* Nigel Rees, *Sayings of the Century*, 1984; Nigel Rees, *Dictionary of Phrase & Allusion*, 1991.)

cowperson: See -PERSON.

[cretin]: See [MENTALLY HANDICAPPED].

[criminal]: See -CHALLENGED and OFFENDER.

[cripple/crippled by] See DISABLED.

cultural imperialism: What MULTICULTURALISM is designed to combat: the domination of one culture by another. By this is usually meant the domination of AFRICAN-AMERICAN culture by EUROCENTRIC culture. However, American culture generally has also been accused of dominating most of the western hemisphere and beyond – as through 'Coca-Cola imperialism', 'Hollywood imperialism', and so on.

> Passions have flamed high this year over Columbus and his blessed or cursed landfall, not just in academic circles but also among curriculum-makers and ethnic interest groups ... Should the word 'discovery' and the expression 'New World' be purged? Is it 'Eurocentric' to honor Columbus? Or, perhaps, anti-Italian to attack him? – *The Washington Post*, 12 October 1991.

> Anyone even suspected of sexism, racism, smoking or cultural imperialism (alleging that, say, Christmas is in some way 'better' than an indigenous Afro-Caribbean feast) is out, out, out. – *The Sunday Telegraph*, 29 December 1991.

culturally different: See ETHNIC MINORITIES.

custody suite: Euphemism for a **[police cell]**, following the Police and Criminal Evidence Bill in January 1986.
See also [PRISONER].

(*Source: Longman Register of New Words*, 1986.)

customer: See RAILSPEAK.

D

date rape: This term arose in the US at the beginning of the 1990s to identify a particular and predominant type of rape – one that involved people who were not strangers, and that took place on a date or during a similarly voluntary encounter.

> He suggested revisions to the screenplay [of *Basic Instinct*] to tone down what appeared to be date rape; to include lines making Douglas's character a politically correct cop who utters, 'A lot of the best people I've met in this town are gay'; and to delete sexist and ageist remarks of an old-time police officer. – *The Washington Post*, 4 June 1991.

> There is nothing new about ending up having sex with someone you didn't quite mean to; but calling it date rape or 'acquaintance rape' is relatively recent. The concept originated in the United States in the Eighties and took hold among the politically correct movement in American universities. – *The Independent*, 20 November 1991.

As with **acquaintance rape** (which equally may occur at any time, and not just on a date) the rape may constitute no more than verbal harassment and not legally recognized rape.

There are some people who object to the actual word 'rape' and for them the search for a PC word to describe the act continues. As Dale Spender wrote in *Man Made Language* (1980), 'A woman who has been attacked in this way has no other name except *rape* to describe the event, but with the inbuilt neutrality of meaning, *rape* is precisely what she does *not* mean ... Women need a word which renames male violence and misogyny and which asserts their blameless nature, a word which places the responsibility where it belongs – on the dominant group.'

[dead]: All the traditional euphemisms for death survive – 'passed away, passed on, gone before, no longer with us' but what has PC put in their place? See -CHALLENGED.

Dead White European Male: See D.W.E.M.

[deaf]: Euphemisms like **[hard of hearing]** – there is also a Welsh expression 'heavy of hearing' – refuse to lie down. The term **impaired hearing** has also been in use for some time:

> Ear phones . . . are the most serviceable present means of aiding impaired hearing. J.F. Barnhill, *Nose, Throat and Ear*, No. 583, 1928.

Deaf and dumb should only be used with caution, if at all. Some deaf people can speak, even if they prefer to converse via sign language.

Profoundly deaf is the term for people who have 'no useful hearing' (presumably what once would have been called 'stone deaf.') Others who have some useful hearing may be described as 'hard of hearing' or 'hearing impaired'. The most PC of terms is probably **with hearing difficulties.** See AURALLY CHALLENGED, AURALLY INCONVENIENCED and -CHALLENGED.

[dear]: As a form of address, the PC Person only uses this word in intimate moments (if at all). At other times, when used to someone (especially female) with whom one is not intimate, it would probably be considered patronizing. Together with **[dearie]**, 'these words are patronizing when used by a man or a woman to someone (usually a woman) who has not overtly or tacitly given permission to be so addressed. In particular, these terms have no business in the workplace or in social interactions with strangers' – Rosalie Maggio, *The Nonsexist Word Finder: A Dictionary of Gender-Free Usage*, Boston, Mass., (1988).

In around 1979, a feminist graffito 'END VIOLENCE TO WOMEN NOW' was daubed in large letters on a wall near Wandsworth gaol, London. In equally large letters, another graffitist, presumably male, subsequently added, 'YES, DEAR'. This was not at all a PC thing to do.

Compare [LOVE].

[dedicated weight-watcher]: See [FAT].

[defective]: See [MENTALLY HANDICAPPED].

[deformed]: See DISABLED.

deprived people: See [POOR].

developing countries: A politically correct term that is used in place of the pejorative **[underdeveloped countries]**. It was in fairly wide usage from at least the mid-1980s.

See also THIRD WORLD, THE.

-different: A construction that is popular with PC jokesmiths, but still lags behind -CHALLENGED. As all the -CHALLENGED jokes sprang from the coinage PHYSICALLY CHALLENGED, so all the -DIFFERENT coinages have grown out of PHYSICALLY DIFFERENT.

Note COSMETICALLY, CULTURALLY, ETHICALLY, MORALLY and PHYSICALLY DIFFERENT and compare all the DIFFERENTLY- coinages here:

differently abled: See -ALBED and DISABLED.

differently advantaged: See [POOR].

differently hirsute: See [BALD/BLADING].

differently interesting: Instead of **[boring]**. See also CHARM-FREE.

(*Source:* Beard & Cerf, *The Official Politically Correct Dictionary and Handbook*, 1992.)

differently pleasured: See [SADO-MASOCHISTIC].

differently heighted: See [SMALL].

differently sized: See [FAT].

differently weighted: See [FAT].

[dike]: See DYKE.

[dirty]: See HYGIENICALLY CHALLENGED.

disabled: There is no aspect of political correctness more challenging than in deciding which words should be used to describe the mentally and physically disabled. When I invited Marlene Pease, producer of BBC Radio's long-running programme *Does He Take Sugar?* (see 'DOES HE TAKE SUGAR?' SYNDROME), to give me her comments on this highly-charged field, she said: 'The language used to describe disability and disabled people is politically volatile and changing so fast that it is almost impossible to keep up ... It is almost impossible to get the terminology right – what suits one person doesn't suit another, but the really negative phrases are **[the disabled]** and the [HANDICAPPED]. We always talk about **disabled people** or **people with disabilities**.'

So that is a start. The reason for choosing these two terms in preference to the previous ones is clearly spelt out in a briefing note entitled 'Improving Media Images of Disability' dated May 1992 and issued by RADAR (the Royal Association for Disability and Rehabilitation): 'Perhaps the chief problem is that disability looms so large in people's minds that it obscures the fact that there is a person there. The terms "the disabled", "the blind", etc. should always be avoided precisely because they focus entirely on the disability and dehumanize the people referred to in this way.'

Other key words and phrases objected to by disabled people (or, more often, by people concerned with looking after them) are **[afflicted by]**, **[crippled by]**, **[deformed]**, **[stricken by]**, [SUFFERER/SUFFERING FROM] and [-VICTIM/VICTIM OF].

Restricting ourselves at this point to physical disabilities (for mental disabilities, see under [MENTALLY HANDICAPPED]), let us consider some of the expressions that are used, some that have been discarded, and others that may be in the process of becoming established. One of the most controversial is the relatively recent coinage **physically different**. This is one of several attempts to get away from the labels of 'handicap' and 'disability' – and especially to avoid the label **[physically handicapped]**.

The society we [people affected by thalidomide] were born into is not adapted to physically different people. – (Speaker on) *David Frost on Sunday*, ITV, 24 July 1988.

Another relative newcomer is **physically challenged**. This is rare among the -CHALLENGED constructions in that it is not simply a joke. Indeed, it may be the example which inspired all the serious and not-so-serious suggestions. Nancy Mairs, an essayist and poet with multiple sclerosis, is one of those who has voiced her opposition to it:

Physically challenged doesn't distinguish me from a woman climbing Mt. Everest. It blurs the distinction between our lives. – *The Washington Post*, 25 August 1991.

A modest proposal put forward in a letter to *The Independent* (25 July 1992) by a wheelchair-user who has multiple sclerosis was **physiologically disenfranchised**.

The construction **person with -** is considered acceptable (for the same reasons as P.W.A.). Hence, consider talking about a 'person with a disability', a 'person who is blind', since it puts the person before the disability. Bear in mind, however, that there are extremists who will argue that there are not (or should not be) such things nowadays as 'disabilities'. They would say that people either have 'different abilities' or 'other abilities'. (See PERSON/ PEOPLE WITH DIFFERING ABILITIES.)

Whatever word you do choose, bear in mind also that the people at the heart of the dispute – those with disabilities – may well disagree with it. Broadly speaking, they are a good deal less sensitive on the subject than many of their carers:

> Virtually no disabled person uses the cute phrases adopted by politically correct wanna-bes. 'The differently abled', the 'handi-capable', the 'physically and mentally challenged' and their ilk are almost universally dismissed as too gimmicky and too inclusive. – *The Washington Post*, 25 August 1991.

A word like **[cripple]**, seemingly offensive and pejorative, is probably non-PC among carers, but as with other negative labels, is not unloved by those who are that way themselves.

> It's not that disabled people are thin-skinned. Indeed, 'crips', 'gimps', 'blinks' and 'deafies' have long been used internally by people with those disabilities. And they can match anyone in constructing euphemisms – among them 'walkies' and 'TABs' (the 'temporarily able-bodied', a you'll-get-yours-yet reminder that disability hits most of us in old age if not before) . . . Surprisingly, a reader survey by [*Disability Rights*] magazine last summer found that some physically disabled people prefer the very word that is the ultimate in offensiveness to others: 'cripple'. – *The Washington Post*, 25 August 1991.

See also [-HANDICAPPED/THE HANDICAPPED]; IMPAIRMENT; PRINT-HANDICAPPED.

(*Sources include:* John Ayto, *The Longman Register of New Words*, 1990; *The Oxford English Dictionary*, Second Edition.)

DISABLISM: Discrimination and prejudice against the disabled. Also written 'disable-ism', 'disableism'. Those who behave in this manner are 'disablist/disable-ist, disableist'.

> I am not apologising for SM and believe that in itself it is neither racist, classist, disablist nor anti-semitic. – *Spare Rib*, May 1986.

disadvantaged people: See [POOR].

DISCLAIMERS: I suppose the practice of authors covering themselves against charges of using pronouns in a sexist manner dates back to the mid-1970s. Certainly by the time I came to write *The Joy of Clichés*, published in 1984, the disclaimer habit was so well-established that I, ironically, put this at the start of my book:

> NOTE: Throughout the book I have used the personal pronoun 'he'. The only reason for this is that it is far less long-winded than writing 'he or she' every time. 'Ladies' should not take offence. They may substitute 'she' if they feel so inclined.

Five years later, authors were still at it, using the same justifications, with or without irony. From Moyra Bremner, *Enquire Within Upon Modern Etiquette* (1989):

> Author's Note. Most of this book applies equally to both sexes. To save my readers from the tedium of repeated 'him or her', 'himself or herself', 'he or she' I have randomized the use of the sexes. Unless it is illogical to the context, for her read him, for him read her, and assume no sexism if a comment seems to be directed at one sex not at both – it is meant to apply equally.

More recently, with less irony, I felt the need to put this at the beginning of my book *Best Behaviour* (1992):

> Author's note. Masculine and feminine nouns and pronouns are used throughout *Best Behaviour* on the basis of appropriateness to the context and, it is to be hoped, overall equality. The reader may substitute the masculine for the feminine, and vice versa, as he or she desires.

Lest any author still thinks that he (*sic*) can get away with putting in a disclaimer to the effect that masculine pronouns are to be taken as applying to women as well, let him beware. Monica Furlong addressed these comments to the editor of *The Author* (Summer 1992 issue):

You defend the offensive practice of claiming at the beginning of a book that masculine pronouns are to apply to both women and men, saying that 'it is the only way of avoiding innumerable infelicities and clumsiness.' But why? It is not necessary to say 'he or she', every time, which *is* clumsy, but it is perfectly possible sometimes to write about 'he' and sometimes about 'she'. If you believe, as I do not, that 'he' stands in perfectly well for 'she', then why should 'she' not stand in perfectly well for 'he'?

The only safe method to adopt is that espoused by the non-sexist language part of 'Guidelines for Factual Programmes (BBC, 1989): 'If he or she or his or her is not acceptable, *change the sentence*.' Usually, this means using a construction including the word 'they'.

[discovery]: In the context of what Christopher Columbus is supposed to have made with regard to America in 1492, this word should, of course, be replaced with a PC reference to **colonization.**

DISEASEISM: Discrimination against the ill. If such a concept does indeed exist today, it was anticipated in Samuel Butler's *Erewhon* (1872). In that delightfully misanthropic work, people who are ill do not get sent to hospital. They get put in *prison* until they are better.

(*Sources include:* Beard & Cerf, *The Official Politically Correct Dictionary and Handbook*, 1992.)

disempowered: In certain New Age and feminist discussions, it is mandatory to speak of being disempowered rather than being **[powerless]**. The logic behind this would seem to be that everyone possesses an innate power which cannot be taken away. So it is impossible to be powerless. However, circumstances or the behaviour of others may prevent you from using your power. Hence, 'I feel disempowered by you' is a useful PC phrase to throw around, even if the meaning is really, 'I don't know what to do in this situation' and 'It's all your fault'.

Hence, 'empowerment', as a way of describing an important process, is also very PC.

[Sandra Bernhard] explains her dancing about in a G-string...as a gesture of empowerment. 'It's like, taking control of your own sexuality – and a kind of "fuck you" to everybody who tells women to do stuff like that. It's saying, "This is a statement, controlled by me".' – *The Independent on Sunday*, 31 August 1992.

[dishonest]: Use **ethically disorient(at)ed** or **morally different.** Compare **morally challenged** under -CHALLENGED.

(*Source:* Beard & Cerf, *The Official Politically Correct Dictionary and Handbook*, 1992.)

'DOES HE TAKE SUGAR?' SYNDROME, THE: A principal failing of people when dealing with the physically disabled is brilliantly encapsulated in the title of the BBC Radio 4 series *Does He Take Sugar?* This phrase, pinpointed originally by social workers in the title of a booklet, 'Does he take sugar in his tea?', has been used since the programme's inception in 1978. It represents the unthinking attitude that leads people to talk to the companions or relatives of those with a physical disability rather than directly to the people themselves.

For the record, it has nothing to do with diabetes. It refers to the tendency of able-bodied people to speak over the heads of those with a disability and assume that they are brain-dead. In fact the vast majority of people, no matter what their disability, are perfectly able and willing to speak for themselves. In particular, we should not assume that people with a mental handicap are inarticulate. – 'Guide to the Representation of People With Disabilities in Programmes' (compiled by Geoffrey Prout, BBC, 1990).

I wonder if anyone in the ranks of the PC has ever objected to the blatant sexism of the title?

dog warden: This replaces the term **[dog catcher]**. Reporting the appointment of an ex-police officer to this task, the *Civic Review*

(Stockport) for November 1978, explained: 'He doesn't want to be regarded as just a dog catcher. As a dog lover he sees his job as one of educator rather than apprehender.'

Compare RODENT OFFICER/OPERATIVE.

(*Source:* Vernon Noble, *Speak Softly – Euphemisms and Such*, 1982.)

domestic assistant: See [CLEANING LADY].

domestic engineer: See HOMEMAKER.

[Doris]: Totally unacceptable name for a (usually) middle-aged woman, especially when used by a police officer – and that's official. A Metropolitan Police handbook entitled *Focusing on Fair Treatment for All* (July 1992) lists this term along with [SPADE] for a black person and [GIRL] as an automatic way of referring to a female officer, as terms to be avoided. Frankly, I always call middle-aged women **[Gladys]**, but . . . whoops!

(*Source: The Independent*, 23 July 1992.)

[down-and-out]: See [TRAMP].

Down's syndrome: The term **[mongolism]** had been used to describe this medical condition since before 1900. *The Oxford English Dictionary* (Second Edition) contains a definition of mongolism that clearly indicates where offence might lie: 'Congenital form of mental deficiency . . . marked by numerous signs, including short stature, short thick hands and feet, a large tongue, a flat face with features somewhat similar to those of Mongolians . . . '

The change of name followed a conscious campaign. A letter to *The Lancet* (8 April 1961), signed by G. Allen and others, contributed to the move: 'Some of the undersigned are inclined to replace the term "mongolism" by such designations as "Langdon-Down anomaly", or "Down's syndrome or anomaly" or "congenital acromicria".' Later in 1961 (21 October), *The Lancet* noted: 'Our contributors prefer Down's syndrome to mongolism because they believe that the term 'mongolism' has misleading racial connotations and is hurtful to many parents' (let alone Mongolians, one might think.) The condition was thus named after J.L.H. Down (1828-96), an English physician who first described the genetic disorder in 1866, and the name-change was quite rapidly adopted by most people, though even now some hesitate slightly before using the newer expression. They are probably more fully aware that they should not say 'mongolism' than why they should invoke the name of a man called Down.

Accordingly, people are said thus to be 'with Down's syndrome' or to be 'Down's syndrome patients' or simply 'Down's people' – but *not*, of course, to be a 'Down's syndrome [SUFFERER]'.

In 1963 Magdalene Wilkins took her infant daughter, Jane, to the John Radcliffe Hospital in Oxford to see a consultant paediatrician ... 'She took one look at Jane and said, "Oh well, you've got a mongol baby".' – *The Independent*, 28 August 1992.

'Evidently they have difficulty placing Down's people in work round here.' – *Ibid*.

[dust(bin)man]: See REFUSE COLLECTOR. Oddly, Val Dumond in *The Elements of Nonsexist Usage* (New York, 1990), recommends 'street sweeper' for the **[dustman]**. As 'dustman' is a mostly British usage anyway, she is probably confusing his or her function with that of **[roadsweeper]** (see STREET ORDERLY).

drug abuse: See -ABUSE.

[drunk]: See [ALCOHOLIC].

[dwarf]: See PERSON OF RESTRICTED GROWTH.

D.W.E.M.: Acronym (pronounced 'DWEM') for a 'Dead White European Male' (though on rare occasions he was just a D.W.M.). DWEMs – of whom one might just mention Shakespeare and Beethoven – are those failure-free, gravestone-enhanced, persons of non-colour who are to blame for the EUROCENTRIC bias of university syllabuses in the US (and, indeed, everywhere).

dyke: *Not* a politically *incorrect* term for a lesbian – nor, for the more mannish type of lesbian in particular, as might have been supposed, though the spelling **[dike]** apparently is. Subdivisions include the PC 'bull dyke', 'butch' and 'femme'.

In the 1980s, some lesbians started defiantly referring to themselves as dykes, possibly because the last thing they wanted to do was to have to share the word GAY with male homosexuals. Before this happened, the term had largely been one of abuse aimed at them and was current by the 1940s at least. The origin of the term is obscure.

> Prigs will do well to stay away from 'Déjàvu' [play by John Osborne]. So will people with politically-correct tendencies who lack a sense of humour. For much of the first act Jimmy Porter sounds like an educated Alf Garnett – or, for Americans, an educated Archie Bunker. He jibes at schools that set Elton John for their O-level examinations. He recites limericks of the sort that begin: 'A black feminist dyke from Khartoum'. – *The Economist*, 13 June 1992.

Compare the defiant use by male homosexuals of **bent** and **queer**.

E

economically exploited/[disadvantaged]: See [POOR, THE].

economical with the truth: See COUNTER-FACTUAL PROPOSITION.

[editrix]: See [-RIX SUFFIX].

[educationally subnormal]: See [MENTALLY HANDICAPPED].

[elderly]: See [OLD].

[Englishman]: According to Val Dumond's *The Elements of Non-sexist Usage* (New York, 1990), the correct term is **English person**. Hence, we may look forward to seeing the title of R.F. Delderfield's novel changed to *God Is an English Person*.

enslaved person: See [SLAVE].

environment(ally) friendly: See -FRIENDLY.

equal opportunity: In the 1970s, this phrase came mostly to refer to employment opportunities for women, and that is how it has remained although, possibly to minimize the POSITIVE DISCRIMINATION often involved, TOKENISM dictates the occasional male application. Originally, as 'equality of opportunity', the term referred to general social mobility. Then, as 'equal opportunity' it seems to have resurfaced in the US with specific reference to racial prejudice and discrimination.

A sufficient measure of social justice, to ensure health, education, and a measure of equality of opportunity. – H.G. Wells, *The Outline of History* (1920).

Equal opportunity for all, under free institutions and equal laws – there is the banner for which we will do battle against all rubber-stamp bureaucracies or dictatorships. – Winston Churchill, *Victory* (1946).

I define integration not as a flattening process of assimilation but as equal opportunity accompanied by cultural diversity in an atmosphere of mutual tolerance. – *The Listener*, 26 December 1968.

N.Y. Hilton ... An equal opportunity employer. – *The New York Times*, 3 November 1972.

Equality of opportunity ... can be glossed as 'equal opportunity to become unequal'. – Raymond Williams, *Keywords* (1976).

'Equal opportunities!' said Norman. 'That's one of the things we men prefer to leave to the ladies!' – Barbara Pym, *Quarter in Autumn* (1977).

Ms Betty Lockwood, Chairman of the Equal Opportunities Commission, told a WEA seminar of trade union officials that positive discrimination inside unions and in training should be encouraged. That means discrimination in favour of either men or women, though in practice it is likely to mean women. – *Film & Television Technician*, 8 March 1977.

The UK Equal Opportunities Commission was established in 1975.

The Thatcherite view accepts the ... thesis that 'equality of opportunity means equal opportunity to be unequal'. – John Boyd-Carpenter, *Way of Life* (1980).

(*Sources include: The Oxford English Dictionary*, Second Edition.)

[Eskimo(s)]: See INNUIT/INUIT.

[ESSEX GIRL JOKES]: A definitely non-PC form of entertainment. In Britain, there was a craze for these jokes in the Autumn of 1991 – sample: 'Q. How does an Essex Girl turn on the light after sex? A. She kicks open the car door.' As such, they were a straight lift of the 'Blonde jokes' that had been popular in the United States shortly before. Sample: 'Q. How can you change a Blonde's mind?' – 'A. Blow in her ear.'

The British type was probably so named on the model of 'Essex Man' – a term describing a prosperous, uncouth, uneducated person who did well out of the Thatcher years and was identified as likely to be found dwelling in Essex (a county just to the east of London).

Feminists are now denouncing the blonde jokes as 'a manifestation of the new misogyny'. Top of their hit-list is a television advertisement for beer which asks: 'Why do gentlemen prefer blondes?' Answer: 'Dumb Question'. 'They aren't politically correct,' said Valerie Strauss, an editor at *The Washington Post*. 'They are dumb woman jokes and there is nothing new about them.' – *The Times*, 7 November 1991.

Not long ago, I worked very briefly at Radio 4, which is a terrifically politically correct sort of place, and one day in the office I told an Essex Girl joke. A young woman there turned on me as if I came from another, less advanced planet, and, more in sorrow than in anger, said she didn't think what I'd said was frightfully right-on . . . [This] is the age of the joyless and the shrivelled. Do Your Own Thing has turned into Not In My Back Yard. – *The Independent*, 23 April 1992.

[-ESS SUFFIX]: Dislike of this suffix stems partly from its sexist typing, hence the preference for the female poet or ACTOR, and partly from the awkward words it can produce. **[Doctress]** never seems to have caught on, though the form was known by 1549; **doctor** seems always to have been applied to medical and doctoral persons of either sex. This does not apply in other languages, of course. Germaine Greer appears to have no objection to being referred to as *dottoressa* by the Italians. **[Authoress]** is also a clumsy word, but not many a female **writer** would insist on **author** these days, given that 'writer' is just as good a word. 'Author' has always been rather pompous anyway. **Adulterer, adventurer, ambassador, conductor, god**, and **steward** are preferred to **[adulteress], [adventuress], [ambassadress], [conductress], [goddess], [stewardess]**. However, **abbess**, 'the use of the feminine form of "abbott" is acceptable. This is one of the few exceptions to the rule about eliminating feminine endings; in most instances abbesses have been the equals of abbots in power, influence, and respect.' – Rosalie Maggio, *The Nonsexist Word Finder: A Dictionary of Gender-Free Usage*, Boston, Mass., 1988.

ethically different: Term for **[corrupt]**. A joke coinage from *The New York Times*, July 1992.

ethically disorient(at)ed: See [DISHONEST].

ethnically challenged: See -CHALLENGED.

ethnic minorities: The key PC phrase for minorities belonging to a particular race or 'differentiated from the rest of the community by racial origins and cultural background' – *The Oxford English Dictionary* (Second Edition). As 'ethnic minority group', the term has been known in the US since the early 1950s. In the UK, since the 1960s, the phrase has been used to refer to immigrants generally – appropriately so, as 'ethnic' has an interesting etymology, from the Greek *ethnos* (nation) *and ethnikos* (heathen).

'Ethnic origin' presumably came to be used as a way of avoiding the word 'race' with its connotations of prejudice and discrimination. 'Ethnic' is now used with utter looseness. It may simply mean 'non-European' or 'foreign'.

Is there not something politically correct about the graffito I saw sprayed on a north London wall this week: Ethnics out? – *The Guardian*, 9 November 1991.

But 'ethnic minority' may have had its day. A **culturally different** group is probably now more correct (*The Times*, 28 June 1992).

[-ETTE SUFFIX]: The addition of '-ette' to any standard (male) word is definitely not PC. Despite the glorious history of the **[suffragette]** movement – that should be **suffragist** - there is an undoubted frivolity about such terms as **[hackette]** (for a female journalist), **[bachelorette]**, and especially **[majorette].**

EUROCENTRIC/ISM/ICITY: These are mostly US terms to describe the educational and cultural obsession with the work of D.W.E.M.S and the consequent failure to appreciate the genius of those nearer home.

exceptional: See [MENTALLY HANDICAPPED].

experientially enhanced: See [OLD].

[extra-large]: See [FAT].

[Eyetie/Iti/Ity]: An offensive term, however you spell it, for an Italian – taken from the humorous pronunciation 'Eyetalian' and in use by 1925.
   Italian is the only correct form. In the US, the term **Italian-American** (which has been around since at least the 1900s) should be used as straightforwardly descriptive of those people who are of Italian descent. On no account should it be used to describe the kind of behaviour associated with 'the Mafia' or with 'organized crime', as that would be to indict a whole community for the activities of but a small part of it.

F

[faggot]: This word for a male homosexual – almost entirely restricted in use to the US – is definitely non-PC, as (unlike QUEER and BENT) it is seldom if ever self-applied (though there was, I believe, a novel called *Faggots* by Larry Kramer in the early 1970s which celebrated the term).

[failure]: See INCOMPLETE SUCCESS.

family butcher: See [BUTCHER].

family name: See [MAIDEN NAME].

family planning: Probably coined as early as 1914 by Mrs Margaret Sanger, an American, this is an example of a positive euphemism – lacking the negative note in the earlier expressions [birth control] and [contraception].

(*Source:* Vernon Noble, *Speak Softly – Euphemisms and Such*, 1982.)

[Fanagalo]: See [KAFFIR].

[fat]: It is unforgivable to use this non-PC word. Attempts have been made for many years to find suitable euphemisms, of course. Mrs Oliphant wrote in *Salem Chapel* (1863) of 'Miss Phoebe' that she was: 'Pink – not red – a softened youthful flush, which was by no means unbecoming to the plump, full-figure which had not an angle anywhere.' But all the traditional euphemisms are non-PC, namely: [bonny], [broad in the beam], [buxom], [dedicated

weight-watcher], [fleshy], [full-figured], [full in the face], [gener-
ously proportioned], [not so slim as one would like to be],
[plump], [putting on weight], [well-built], [well-endowed], [with
a mature figure], [with surplus weight] – all because they are not
'political' enough and do not present sufficiently POSITIVE IMAGES.
[Adipose], [obese] and [stout] are too direct.

> [Social] workers often hold common biases . . . an unconscious
> rejection of very obese clients. – Claudia L. Jewett, *Adopting the
> Older Child*, Boston, Mass., 1978.

[Outsize(d)], also, has a too critical edge to it. Michael Barratt
talking about a slimming competition on the BBC TV programme
Nationwide (3 May 1977) used the word [over-shapely], but this is
verging on the humorous, not to say patronizing, and thus cannot
qualify for PC-dom. Big remains a borderline case, only to be used
with sensitivity.

So what is the PC term? Differently sized appears to be the front-
running substitute at the moment, with differently weighted somewhat to the rear. Or you can talk about a person with an alternative
body image:

> [In the US] it is unacceptable to describe even a 38-stone man as
> fat. All you can say is that he has 'an alternative body image'. –
> *The Times*, 19 April 1992.

Also in the US, horizontally challenged, larger than average,
person of size, and person of substance may be spoken with a
straight face.

In clothing matters, for [extra-large] it is probably in order to
substitute generously cut despite what I have said about [gener-
ously proportioned] above.

(*Sources include:* Vernon Noble, *Speak Softly – Euphemisms and Such*, 1982;
Beard & Cerf, *The Official Politically Correct Dictionary and Handbook*, 1992; *The
Times*, 13 April 1992.)

FATIST/FATTIST: See FATISM.

FATISM/FATTISM/FATTYISM: Unfair discrimination and prejudice against fat, overweight people. In the form 'fattism', the word was coined by an American psychologist, Rita Freedman, in her book *Bodylove* (1988), but the notion was not new.

Fatist is a refreshing new word to me, as opposed to fattest which is much more familiar. – *Spare Rib*, October 1987.

Grange Hill ... – the programme that single-handedly convinces entire generations of schoolchildren that they aren't *living* unless their classrooms resound with parody, criminalspeak, uninventive abuse, bullying, racism and fattyism. – *The Observer*, 10 April 1988.

Mr Lawson has been the subject of grossly fattist caricatures in the popular prints, especially this week. Who would wish to see new laws to ban such discrimination? – *The Daily Telegraph*, 17 March 1989.

Women weigh into 'fatist' oppressors . . . At 5ft 2in tall and weighing 16st, one of the organisers, Miss Ruth Teddern, had a number of grievances to air against the 'fat-ists' who think fat people are there purely as a source of amusement. – *The Sunday Telegraph*, 19 March 1989.

Uncertainty over the spelling continues to dog the expression:

BILLY BUNTER IS 'FATIST' SAY BBC. – Headline, *The Sun*, 9 September 1992.

Bunter's a fattist bounder. – Headline, *The Daily Mirror*, 9 September 1992.

Interestingly, however, the story referred to in these headlines introduces an alternative name (probably a nonce-word) – **STOUT-ISM** – for the prejudice:

The Owl of the Remove has been given the old heave-ho for being stoutist, racist and not politically correct . . . Mikael Shields, of BBC Enterprises, said: 'Children are far quicker than adults at spotting and rejecting cases of racism and stoutism.' – *The Daily Mirror*, 9 September 1992.

Caution should be exercised with these coinages, as both 'fatism' and 'stoutism' contain the non-PC elements [FAT] and [stout].

Compare WEIGHTISM.

(*Sources include: The Longman Register of New Words*, 1990; *The Oxford Dictionary of New Words*, 1991.)

feel good: Your reward for behaving and speaking in a politically correct manner is that you 'feel good'. In consequence, 'feeling good with yourself' is a way of describing your 'quality of life' – indeed, it is the name given to a whole mystique. The term pre-dates PC:

> Then there are the 'Mr Feel Good' labels. These assure you a position in lefty heaven because you have bought yogurt from Fred, 'made with loving care and pure Jersey milk from a nearby farm' or politically-correct coffee beans made by workers in Nicaragua who will never use Hair Salad on contras. – *The Washington Post*, 27 December 1987.

> [A] way to get patients under control without bullying them . . . Invented by the hippy generation in the Sixties and developed later by the advertising industry, 'feel good' techniques such as assertiveness training and counselling are designed to reassure customers such as airline passengers and patients that they are in control of situations over which patently they have not the slightest influence. – *The Daily Telegraph*, 21 April 1992.

femhole: What the good feminist says, should he or she ever have occasion to draw attention to a **[manhole]**. The word was coined by Bina Goldfield in *The Efemcipated English Handbook* (1983), but should only be used in moments of extreme protest. **Personhole** is much more straight down the middle. Other terms include 'sewer/ utility/access hole' and 'utility access hole'.

(*Sources include:* Rosalie Maggio, *The Nonsexist Word Finder: A Dictionary of Gender-Free Usage*, Boston, Mass., 1988.)

FEMINISM/FEMINIST: The advocacy of women's rights and the person who advocates them – and so known since at least the 1890s.

femstruate: Always use in preference to **[menstruate]** which contains the most unfortunate 'men' intrusion. 'Femstruate' is another of Bina Goldfield's coinages from *The Efemcipated English Handbook* (1983) and it is regretted that no gender-free substitute has been found for this word. Rosalie Maggio, however, in *The Nonsexist Word Finder* (1988) is quite happy with 'menses/menstrual', labelling the the words 'non-sexist', as 'menses' is merely Latin for 'months'.

Filipino: A person originating from the Philippines. In 1988, the *Oxford English Dictionary* came in for a good deal of misplaced abuse in the Philippines themselves because it was thought to contain the definition, *'Filipina* – a domestic help'. But it did not – and does not. When challenged on this point, Victor Lim, president of the Philippine Chamber of Commerce, who had lodged the original complaint, backtracked slightly and said, 'It might have been Webster.' But it is not there either. As I am always saying, the price of pedantry is eternal vigilance, and that goes for political correctness, too.

(*Source: The Independent*, 18 November 1988.)

financially challenged: See -CHALLENGED.

firefighter: Mandatory substitution for **[fireman]**. 'The overwhelming majority are male but fire-fighters and fire crews will usually do the job' – 'Guidelines for Factual Programmes', BBC (1989).

[First Lady]: i.e. the spouse of the US President. The first 'first Lady of the Land' to be so called may have been the wife of Abraham

Lincoln, who was mentioned thus by William Howard Russell in 1863. Clearly not PC nowadays. The spouse of the President should simply be referred to as 'Ms' or 'Mrs' (until such time as there is a male one, that is). On the other hand, Hillary Clinton was making it known that she would wish to be known as the **Presidential Partner** even before her husband was elected in November 1992.

(*Sources include:* Val Dumond, *The Elements of Nonsexist Usage*, New York, 1990.)

first name: See [CHRISTIAN NAME].

fleshy: See [FAT].

flier: See [AIRMAN/AIRWOMAN].

flight attendant: This is the completely non-sexist version of the acceptable **airline steward** and the utterly unacceptable **[airline stewardess]**, even though it has unfortunate echoes of 'lavatory attendant' (for which, curiously, there never seems to have been a politically incorrect term). Flight attendant was in use by the late 1940s.

Flying Dutchperson: See -PERSON.

follicularly challenged: See -CHALLENGED.

[freak]: See [MENTALLY HANDICAPPED].

-FREE: A suffix denoting the employment of right-on methods of production or the absence of a disapproved-of element. Hence, **additive-free** (by 1984), meaning, free from artificial food-additives, and **animal-free** (by 1986), meaning, not using or containing product from animals.

The A.L.P. [Australian Labor Party] supported moves to establish a 'nuclear-free Zone'. – *Annual Register*, 1964.

The Saudis have oil, which the world wants. Now C. Schmidt & Sons, a Philadelphia brewery, has something the Saudis want – alcohol-free beer. – *The Washington Post*, 23 June 1979.

Last week Peter turned up at Broadcasting House with the first ever commercially produced non-sweetened, additive-free yoghurt. – *The Listener*, 10 May 1984.

(*Sources include: The Oxford Dictionary of New Words*, 1991.)

-FRIENDLY: A widely used suffix adopted from computing. 'User-friendly' was current by 1979 and may have been coined by Harlan Crowder 'to represent the inherent ease (or lack of ease) which is encountered in the running of a computer system'. Now means 'assisting, promoting, or in sympathy with a PC cause'. Hence **environment friendly, environmentally friendly** (and the similar constructions: **environmentally aware, environmentally sensitive,** and **environmentally sound.**)

One has to be reasonable. The factory means jobs. There is no factory without emissions. It just has to be as environmentally friendly as possible. – *The Christian Science Monitor*, 6 April 1984.

[full-figured]: See [FAT].

[full in the face]: See [FAT].

[fuzzy-wuzzy]: An absolutely unprintable and unspeakable non-PC term from the days of Empire (current by 1892, at least). The sort of word that Mr Boutros Boutros-Ghali, the Secretary-General of the United Nations, is all too likely to apply to himself (see [WOG]). Nevertheless, the following words appeared written on the screen in the film *The Four Feathers* (1939): 'The Khalifa's army of dervishes and fuzzy-wuzzies masses on the Nile.' Indeed, the term was originally coined for the Sudanese who had a distinctive hair style, and then was applied to natives of other, mostly African, countries.

G

gay: It was at the end of the 1960s that homosexuals (male and female) most noticeably took unto themselves the word 'gay'. This was at a time when the US Gay Liberation Front came 'out of the closet' and used such slogans as 'Glad to be Gay', 'Say it loud, we're gay and we're proud' and '2-4-6-8, gay is just as good as straight'.

However the word 'gay' had been used in this sense, in homosexual circles, since at least the 1930s and on both sides of the Atlantic. In the last century, 'gay' was used to describe female prostitutes and there is an even earlier use of the word applied to female licentiousness. It may (like the word 'camp') have gravitated towards its homosexual use from that.

The French still manage to distinguish between the old and new meanings of the word (at least when writing): 'gay or joyful' is still *gai*; 'gay as homosexual' is *gay*. In English, however, mild confusion still exists:

> 'I had been aware for many years that my sexuality was different from that envisaged by traditional Judaism and tried to ignore it . . .' said Rabbi Solomon. 'But since I've begun to accept that I am gay, I've become a happier person.' – *The Daily Telegraph*, 29 August 1992.

Although one might regret the loss of the word to mean 'joyful, lighthearted', the coinage goes some way towards making up for the pejorative use of **queer** (by 1922) and **bent** (by 1957), to describe homosexuals. **Poof** (also **pouf, poove, poofdah** and the Australian **poofter**) dates back at least to the 1850s, and **puff** (pointing to the likely origin) was apparently tramps' slang for homosexual by

1870. *Private Eye* certainly popularized 'poof' in the 1960s but clearly did not invent it, as has been claimed, though possibly it did coin the 'poove' version.

I may be a poove but I'm a terrific engineer. – *Private Eye*, 30 November 1962.

Apart from [FAGGOT], I am not designating any of these terms politically incorrect as homosexuals quite often take delight in applying such derogatory terms to themselves.

Young American homosexuals want to be called queer rather than gay because it has more 'political potency'. They chant at rallies: 'We're here, we're queer – get used to it.' The trend, led by Militants Queer Nation, is also set to sweep Britain. Lesbian, Liza Powers, 34, said: 'Using a word that is offensive is a way of showing anger. Gay is white middle class.' – *The Sun*, 9 April 1991.

Just when the message had finally got through to the shires, queer is back, this time appropriated by gay people themselves in a development known as the New Queer Politics. Suddenly, gay is bourgeois, it's boring, it's the politics of compromise and reaction. Queer is where it's at. – *The Guardian*, 23 June 1992.

In the summer of 1992, at a Promenade Concert in the Royal Albert Hall, London, I spotted a man wearing a T-shirt emblazoned with the slogan 'Queer to Eternity'.
Not everyone seems capable of going along with this, however:

All 21 of [Enid Blyton's] Famous Five adventures are being published in an updated, bowdlerised edition . . . Blyton's frequently-used adjective 'queer' has given way to 'strange/peculiar/funny/odd'. – *The Observer*, 6 September 1992.

In Egypt in 1989, I encountered the term **special man** used about male homosexuals. Although spoken in a slightly mocking way, it now strikes me as an utterly PC phrase, should anyone care to take it up – though 'person' or 'adult male' would, of course, be better than 'man'.

By the late 1970s, some female homosexuals were rejecting the word 'gay'. There never appears to have been a euphemism for **lesbian** acceptable to them or to others. 'I prefer to reserve the term lesbian to describe women who are woman-identified, having rejected the false loyalties to men on all levels,' wrote Mary Daly in *Gyn/Ecology* (London, 1979). 'The terms gay or female homosexual more accurately describe women who, although they relate genitally to women, give their allegiance to men and male myths, ideologies, styles, practices, and professions.'

A global term **LBG** has also been introduced – standing for 'Lesbians, Bisexuals and Gays' – because to call them all gays would be to 'discriminate against women and bisexuals' (*The Times*, 28 June 1992). The term **[homosexual]** has also fallen out of favour with gays and lesbians because they feel it is 'alien, clinical, and much too limiting to properly denote a whole life-style' (a 1986 view cited in Rosalie Maggio's *The Nonsexist Word Finder: A Dictionary of Gender-Free Usage*, Boston, Mass., 1988.)

See also [HOMO(S)] and [HOMOSEXUALIST].

(*Sources include:* Nigel Rees, *Why Do We Say...?*, 1987; Jane Mills, *Womanwords*, 1991; Nigel Rees, *Dictionary of Phrase & Allusion*, 1991.)

gender, person of: See PERSON OF GENDER.

GENDERISM: The non-sexist name for SEXISM. When distinguishing a person's sex, the word 'gender' is apparently preferred in order to keep the irrelevant associations of 'sex' out of it. Or, rather, the distinction in PC-ish theory is that gender is culturally constructed whereas sex is simply biological.

Gender is the cultural notion of what it is to be a woman or a man. Words like *masculine* and *feminine* describe these notions. In our society we describe people as womanly or manly, as a tomboy or a sissy, as unfeminine or unmasculine. These words have nothing to do with a person's sex; they are culturally acquired, subjective concepts about character traits and expected behaviors that vary from one place to another, from one individual to another. *Gender is cultural.'* – Rosalie Maggio, *The Nonsexist Word Finder: A Dictionary of Gender-Free Usage*, Boston, Mass., (1988).

[In the film *Robin Hood Prince of Thieves*] Maid Marian, we learn appears as a model feminist. Robin has a black lieutenant. The gang set about enforcing correct attitudes on equal rights, genderism, speciesism and religious freedom. – *The Daily Telegraph*, 18 June 1991.

gender reassignment: See [SEX CHANGE].

generously cut: See [FAT].

[generously proportioned]: See [FAT].

[gentleman of the road]: See [TRAMP].

[girl(s)]: These words for a pre-pubertal person should be replaced by **pre-woman** and **pre-women** – except that this was a joke coinage by the American cartoonist Jeff Sheshol in his strip 'Politically Correct Person' (by 1990).

Imagine the shift a children's tale would have to undergo to rid itself of all offending elements. '"It's raining nonhuman animal companions,' said Wendy and Melissa's father.' 'Why don't you prewomen have an herbal tea party for your nonsexist dolls, and then we'll bake some gingerbread persons!' *The Washington Post*, 8 June 1992, quoting Beard & Cerf, *The Official Politically Correct Dictionary and Handbook*, 1992.

See also [DORIS].

(*Sources include: Newsweek*, 24 December 1990.)

[Gladys]: See [DORIS].

God/god: In June 1992 the Methodist Church became 'the first major denomination' to adopt non-sexist language. Its annual conference embraced a concept of a 'God without sexual bias', yet one which would allow talk of 'God the Mother' or 'God our Mother'. The conference only narrowly rejected making a 'balanced-gender liturgy' compulsory. This 'intrusive language' combining male and female images of God was designed to counter what a report drawn up for the church had identified as 'traditional God-talk ... legitimising and perpetuating the power and privilege of males.'

Earlier, Parliament was told in October 1991 that any clergyperson referring to God as 'Our Mother and Father' in the Lord's Prayer would be breaking the law.

As for the pronoun **[He]** when used to refer to God, its days are surely numbered.

So when Methodists turn 'politically correct', it is more in order to avoid hurt feelings than because there has been a theological revelation into the nature of truth. The proposal in their latest report urging that God be called 'She' as well as 'He', is put forward in order to avoid women feeling excluded. – *The Times*, 23 May 1992.

Quite the most appealing and sensible stance from a religious *and* non-sexist point of view is that 'in God there is no gender as we know it. It is acceptable, indeed even more fruitful, to use anthropomorphic metaphors for God that embrace both sexes (God as abundant mother, as merciful father) ... However, God is neither a "he" nor a "she".' – Rosalie Maggio, *The Nonsexist Word Finder: A Dictionary of Gender-Free Usage*, Boston, Mass., (1988). Maggio goes on to note that a list of '196 inclusive names, titles, and phrases referring to God' has been drawn up by an organization called The Coordinating Center for Women in Church and Society in St Louis, Missouri. These include: 'the Almighty, Creator of all Things, the Deity, the Eternal, God of Heaven, Good Parent, Guide, the Holy

One, the Most High, Omnipotent One, Ruler, Savior, Shepherd, Source of Life, and Supreme Being.'

See also -ESS SUFFIX.

(*Sources include: The Daily Telegraph*, 22 October 1991 & 30 June 1992; *The Guardian*, 30 June 1992.)

golden-ager: See [OLD].

GREEN-: Concerned with the conservation of the environment, particularly as a political issue; ecological. The word comes from the German *grün*, as applied to environmental issues by political lobbyists in what was then West Germany in the early 1970s. Now widely used beyond politics (as, for instance, in the colour-coding used to denote lead-free petrol) and in any number of combinations.

'Green' bans have been introduced by the New South Wales Building and Construction Workers' Union. – *The Courier-Mail* (Brisbane), 4 June 1973.

Mr Cramond said that the Highlands welcomed people from outside with knowledge and expertise who were willing to make things work, but there was no room for green settlers who hoped to live on 'free-range' carrots. – *The Aberdeen Press & Journal*, 17 June 1986.

[guard]: See RAILSPEAK.

gynaecologically challenged: See -CHALLENGED.

GYN(A)EPHOBE/GYN(A)EPHOBIA: Woman-hater/fear and hatred of women.

[In the TV series *thirtysomething*] the single folk were always, always unhappy. Ellen, for example, with her husky voice and hapless ways with the fellas could make you . . . gynephobic. – *The Independent*, 29 May 1991.

[gypsy]: Gypsies have been known as **travellers** or **travelling people** since the eighteenth century at least and it is their own name for themselves. But the term 'traveller' has also been applied, not least by themselves, to other types – tinkers, beggars, tramps and vagrants – who are not ethnically Romany. In recent years, wandering groups of hippies have also tended to be termed travellers by the media.

The Government last night pledged new laws to control travellers, as the last hippies evicted from an illegal festival site at Otterbourne, Hampshire, packed up and left, leaving behind a £1m bill for damages. – *The Independent*, 11 August 1992.

I wonder what view traditional travellers have of their word being applied to these newcomers? On the other hand, it appears that proper gypsies do not mind being called 'gypsies'. Indeed, they have good reason to hold on to the name.

Of all those who live in caravans in Britain, gypsies are the only ones that have the distinction of being recognized as an ethnic group and thus protected from discrimination under the 1976 Race Relations Act. Their small victory was the result of a Court of Appeal ruling in 1989 which made this distinction after a pub in Hackney, east London, put a sign on the door banning travellers. Travellers were not held to be an ethnic group, but gypsies were, so the sign was deemed discriminatory. – *The Independent*, 21 August 1992.

H

[hackette]: See [-ETTE SUFFIX].

hair disadvantaged: See [BALD/BALDING].

HAIRISM: Discrimination or prejudice against people on the grounds of hair colour (usually), though hair length might come into it. Consider what happens to women who are [BLONDE] and see [ESSEX GIRL JOKES].

> Joseph Boskin, a Boston professor and author of *Rebellious Laughter: Change and Humour in America*, said: 'The blonde-jokes are a continuation of the first reaction against feminism that started in the late 1970s.' A new offence is being added to the criminal code of the politically correct: hairism. – *The Times*, 29 January 1992.

handi-capable: See next entry.

[-handicapped/the handicapped]: Meaning, with a mental or physical disability. Disapproval of the word 'handicap' on the grounds that it alludes to being 'cap in hand' is questionable etymology. While it is true that 'handicap' in this sense derives from 'handicap' in the sporting sense of a 'disadvantage imposed on a competitor to make the chances more equal', the origin of this word has something obscurely to do with a 'hand i' cap' or 'hand in the cap'.

Referring to physical and mental disabilities, especially in children, the word has been used since at least the 1910s. The words

inconvenienced and **handi-capable** are sometimes employed to put a more positive slant on the problem, though whether 'inconvenienced' can be considered more positive is hard to say.

If anything 'the handicapped' is worse than 'the disabled' as a blanket term because handicap can only be assessed in individual cases. It should not be used. – 'Guide to the Representation of People With Disabilities in Programmes' (compiled by Geoffrey Prout, BBC, 1990).

The word 'handicapped' carries powerful associations of disabled people as passive objects of charity, rather than individuals. – Briefing Note, The Royal Association for Disability and Rehabilitation, May 1992.

See also DISABLED and [MENTALLY HANDICAPPED].

HANDICAPPISM: Discrimination and prejudice against the handicapped – a concept noted by *The Guardian*, 11 June 1986.

HANDISM: Discrimination and prejudice against left-handed people. This takes the form of assuming that everybody is right-handed and failing to make gadgets etc. easily usable by the left-handed.

[hard of hearing]: See AURALLY INCONVENIENCED and [DEAF].

[He]: See GOD.

HEIGHTISM: Discrimination and prejudice against (usually) tall women and short men – though it could be the other way round.

The brand-new 'ism' ... comes from the United States. Speaking as a 5ft 11in female, 'heightism' is something I've suffered from most of my life. – *Good Housekeeping*, February 1988.

heroin abuse: See -ABUSE.

herstory: A word coined by US feminists in the early 1970s as a way of removing the imagined male element from the term **[history]**. The 'his' in 'history' has nothing to do with masculinity, but the new term was adopted as a way of pointing out masculinist tendencies in the writing and teaching of history and its usual preoccupation with male historical figures.

> The fluidity and wit of the witches is evident in the ever-changing acronym: the basic, original title was Women's International Terrorist Conspiracy from Hell . . . and the latest heard at this writing is Women Inspired to Commit Herstory. – Robin Morgan, *Sisterhood is Powerful* (1970).

> I have tried to write a herstory of the inner psychic meaning of the ancient religion. – *Peace News*, 2 October 1981.

(*Sources include: The Oxford Dictionary of New Words*, 1991.)

HETEROSEXISM: Discrimination and prejudice (from a heterosexual) on the grounds of another person's homosexuality; taking the position that heterosexuality is the only acceptable type of sexual orientation.

> Heterosexist language, like so many of the social diseases that require radical treatment, must be understood to be, in and of itself, one of the few manifest symptoms of a thorough-going systemic corruption of human intelligence . . . Heterosexism . . . prescribes that the proper conduct for wimmin is passivity, servility, domicility . . . heterosexuality as the only 'natural' sexual interest. – Julia Penelope, in a paper given to the National Council of Teachers of English convention, San Francisco, November 1979.

(*Source: The Oxford Dictionary of New Words*, 1991.)

HETEROSEXIST: One who practises HETEROSEXISM.

HETEROSEXUAL IMPERIALISM: Another way of expressing HETEROSEXISM. Compare PENILE IMPERIALISM.

Hispanic: The PC term for **Spanish-speaking** people or people of Spanish-American origin, especially in the United States – the latter since the 1970s:

> Remembering his own tough years growing up on the streets in a black-Hispanic neighborhood, Tony DeSando feels close to the problems he and Beth see as the advisers to their church's junior-high group. – Claudia L. Jewett, *Adopting the Older Child* (Boston, 1978).

> Mr Clinton seeking votes during an address to the National Hispanic Leadership Agenda in Washington. According to the Census Department, 29 per cent of Hispanics live below the poverty line. – Picture caption, *The Independent*, 4 September 1992.

The pejorative term **[spic]** (also **[spik]**) for Spanish-speaking people anywhere sounds like a contraction of 'Spanish-speaking' or 'hispanic', but apparently it is not. The journal *American English* suggested, rather, in 1938, that the word came from **[spiggoty]** (various spellings), an abusive term for Spanish-speakers in Central and South America (*c* 1900). When the Panama Canal was being constructed (1901-4), Panamanians would say: 'No spikee de English' and 'spikee de' became 'spiggoty'.

Wentworth & Flexner's *The Dictionary of American Slang* (1975) adds that, in the US, 'spic' has also been applied to Italians or Italian-Americans and derives from 'spaghetti . . . reinforced by the traditional phrase "No spika da English".' Rodgers and Hart had a song (1939) 'Spick and Spanish' whose title might be taken to suggest, misleadingly, that the word has some connection with 'spick and span (new)', meaning 'fresh, tidy, smart'.

> Ring . . . steamed down here on his gunboat just in time to fire that shell and throw a scare into the spiggotys at the very physicky moment. – 'W. Lawton', *Boy Aviators in Nicaragua* (1910).

> It was my first entrance into the land of the panameños, technically known on the Zone as 'spigoties'. – H.A. Franck, *Zone Policeman* (1913).

'He's a spic!' he said. He was frantic with jealousy. – F. Scott Fitzgerald, *Tender Is the Night* (1953 edition).

The term **Hispanic American** may now be used of *any* Spanish-speaking person in North America but usually applies to a person of Latin-American descent.

(*Sources include: The Oxford English Dictionary* (Second Edition); Nigel Rees, *Why Do We Say. . . ?*, Blandford Press, 1987; Nigel Rees, *Dictionary of Phrase & Allusion*, 1991.)

[history]: See HERSTORY.

homemaker: An old word (around since the 1870s at least) which since the late 1970s has been the politically correct term for a **[housewife]** – than which there is no worse label in feminist eyes, particularly when self-applied ('What do you do?' – 'Oh, I'm just a housewife, you know . . .').

Householder is another acceptable term but it is not clear whether it has caught on to any noticeable extent. The male term **househusband** has, against all the odds, gained a good deal of currency (though often uttered a touch self-consciously) to describe the relatively novel situation of a man running a household and looking after the children while his partner goes out to work. **Domestic engineer** has never caught on, for obvious reasons.

The Good Negotiator? What's this? A politically correct update of depressing old usage, which no more enhances domesticity than putting 'home-maker' in your passport? Not at all. The housewife's near-demise is official. A sharp-eyed couple of advertising executives, Daryl Fielding and Cathy Clift of Lowe Howard-Spink, claim to have identified a new domestic breed and named it appropriately. – *The Guardian*, 18 September 1991.

As working novelist, professor and house-husband (his wife, Maureen Quilligan, is a professor of Renaissance studies at the University of Pennsylvania), he could lead a life of his own design. He could work all night when he wanted to. He could pick up his daughter after school. If he had any complaint, it was that he was a little lonely working at home. – *The Washington Post*, 7 February 1992.

'Would you say that to Arthur Miller, who wrote two plays? Would you say: "You chose to be a home-maker" to him? I've written two books,' [Barbara Bush] snapped. – *The Independent*, 21 August 1992.

In appropriate contexts, **consumer** or **shopper** are also preferable to [housewife] – at least according to the BBC 'Guidelines for Factual Programmes' (1989).

HOMOPHOBE/HOMOPHOBIA: A 'homophobe' is someone who is hostile towards or fears homosexuals and the word suddenly became popular in the UK about 1985, particularly as causes of the AIDS problem were discussed. The term 'homophobia' had earlier been popularized by the American writer George Weinberg during the 1970s.

Mock-Wildean aphorisms ('It must be very odd to be a straight man') which are meant to be impossible to swallow are matched against simple, incontrovertible pleas for compassion; memories of sex so positive that they ache are spliced with the hatred of homophobes. – *The Observer*, 17 May 1992.

(*Sources include: The Oxford Dictionary of New Words, 1991.*)

[homo(s)]: Homosexual(s) – a dubious term since the 1920s at least, though quite often used by male homosexuals themselves, e.g. Quentin Crisp ('I became one of the stately homos of England' – *The Naked Civil Servant*, 1968). For some, the word became quite unusable following a curious incident in the early 1960s involving the then Director-General of the BBC, Hugh Carleton-Greene. A memo of a meeting at which Greene had suggested that 'homosexual' should, given its Greek origin, be pronounced with an initial short 'o', was leaked to the press and the suggestion came to be treated as if it was binding on BBC speakers. 'Hommo' lacked whatever it was that 'home-o' had, either in pejorative or self-congratulatory use.

[homosexual]: See GAY.

[homosexualist]: A pejorative way of referring to a homosexual, much used by *Private Eye* from the late 1970s onwards. The *Oxford English Dictionary* (Second Edition) has, however, an example of the word being used in the 1930s.

[honky/honkey/honkie]: Just to show that political correctness in matters of race can cut both ways, let it be stated that the black slang expression for a white person is every bit as offensive as some of the white terms for blacks.

> Many blacks ... came to see it [the African-American Institute] as a 'honky' (white) conservative force. – *The Guardian*, 1 May 1971.

'Disparaging in all uses', states the *Oxford English Dictionary* (Second Edition), and wonders whether it is derived from 'hunky'. It has been current since the 1950s at least. Stuart Berg Flexner in *I Hear America Talking* thinks the word comes 'from the Whites' nasal tone, but some say it originated in Detroit and was first applied to the White men who picked up their Black girlfriends by sitting in their cars and honking the horn in front of the houses where the girls worked as maids'.

What, if any, is the PC term for a white person? Curiously, there isn't one, though wags have suggested **person of non-colour.**

honorary ethnics: A way of referring to women and gays as though they shared the same oppression as ethnic minorities. From the US.

(*Source: The Guardian Weekly*, 26 May 1991.)

horizontally challenged: See -CHALLENGED.

household non-human animal: See ANIMAL COMPANION.

housekeeper: See [CHAMBERMAID].

[housewife] See HOMEMAKER.

HUEISM: This is an invention of my own to describe racial prejudice and discrimination through paint colours.

> In [the film *Bugsy*], limos are black, cars are red and taxis are yellow; all are ominous objects, the NAACP [National Association for the Advancement of Colored People] says, in colours associated with racial minorities. Political correctness, just as we suspected, will be perfectly grey. – *The Daily Telegraph*, 9 April 1992.

[human]: Should not be left at that: say **human animal.** Coming from the Latin *homo* meaning 'human being', this word 'has been used as a noun since 1533 and is used and perceived today as an inclusive term, although most of its dictionary definitions unfortunately include the words "man/men" instead of the correct "human being(s)" ' – Rosalie Maggio, *The Nonsexist Word Finder: A Dictionary of Gender-Free Usage*, Boston, Mass., (1988).

humankind: See [MANKIND].

humorously challenged: See -CHALLENGED.

[hunger]: Consider **nutritional shortfall** – a joke coinage from *The New York Times*, July 1992.

hygienically challenged: For **[dirty]** or **[smelly].** A nonce phrase waiting to be coined. Compare the less-than-PC coinage **[hygienically wanting]** – (the -wanting suffix is not acceptable, as this condition may result from poverty or some other cause for which whatever is so described is not responsible):

> Politically correct washing-up liquid gave us plates that were found hygienically wanting compared with your grandmother's kitchen floor. – *The Independent*, 10 March 1992.

See also -CHALLENGED.

I

ideologically challenged: See -CHALLENGED.

ideological soundness: An alternative name for political correctness. To my way of thinking a more explicit and more honest term, **ideological purity** less so.

> AT&T proudly claims the Basquiat show will be the first retrospective of a black American artist to be mounted at the Whitney Museum of American Art, a New York institution frequently criticized for its pursuit of ideological soundness . . . and its retreat from anything resembling traditional curatorial standards. – *The Economist*, 20 June 1992.

[ike(y)(mo)]: See JEWISH.

[illegitimate]: See -CHALLENGED.

[imbecile]: See [MENTALLY HANDICAPPED].

[immigrant]: In the UK, this has been used to refer specifically to West Indians and Asians. Not least of the reasons for avoiding the term is because many of the people who tend to be so described are not now immigrants but the children of immigrants. They were born here. The PC term would probably be an **ethnic**.

[immigrant Australian]: See ABORIGINAL/ABORIGINE.

impaired hearing: See [DEAF].

impairment: A word to be used with caution, particularly in relation to 'disability' and 'handicap'. These three words are often used interchangeably, but according to the World Health Organization: 'Impairment refers to having a limb, organ or mechanism of the body which is missing or doesn't work properly. Disability is the resulting lack of function. Handicap refers to the limitations on day-to-day activity that result from the disability. Thus, someone may have impaired hearing, and be disabled because they cannot hear voices clearly. The degree of handicap will depend on how effectively a hearing-aid compensates for this.'

(*Source:* 'Guide to the Representation of People With Disabilities in Programmes', compiled by Geoffrey Prout, BBC, 1990.)

INAPPROPRIATELY DIRECTED LAUGHTER: A concept identified at the University of Connecticut and referring to jokes about women, gays or ethnics, for example.

The University of Connecticut ... sought to ban 'inappropriately directed laughter, inconsiderate jokes . . . and conspicuous exclusions (of others) from conversations'. The University of Michigan published material warning students that they could be brought up on charges of laughing at ethnic jokes, questioning the equal ability of men and women to perform certain tasks or excluding an individual from a dorm party because of his sexual orientation. – *The Washington Post*, 17 March 1991.

INCLUSIVE: A PC term referring to language that does not exclude, by direct reference or implication, one gender, minority, group, or another. It is a word most usually employed to denote non-sexist language and has been used in the US since the late 1970s. Behaviour and thought may also, of course, be inclusive or exclusive.

With particular reference to non-sexist language in religion, an *Inclusive Language Lectionary* has been available in the US since 1983. In Britain, the Liturgical Commission of the Church of England is inquiring whether women wish to go on being addressed by such non-inclusive terms as 'Brethren'.

(*Sources: The Oxford Dictionary of New Words*, 1991; *The Author*, Summer 1992.)

incomplete success: That is to say **[failure]**. President Carter used the term in 1980 to describe an attempt to free American hostages held in Iran.

inconvenienced: See [-HANDICAPPED].

indigenous peoples: See [NATIVES].

[-infected]: See [-VICTIM].

infertile: See [BARREN].

Innuit/Inuit: This has always been the way in which **[Eskimo(s)]** have referred to themselves. The word means simply 'people' or 'men' and is variously pronounced, though an 1860 citation gives 'enn-oo-eet'. The Innuit are a people spread over an area from Greenland to eastern Siberia.

Beard & Cerf in their *The Official Politically Correct Dictionary and Handbook* (1992) prefer the spelling 'Inuit', say the word refers specifically to Canadian Eskimos, and attribute Inuit dislike of the word to the fact that they once believed it meant 'eater of raw meat'. For the appropriate sub-division, they recommend the use of Native Alaskan.

> Prime Minister Brian Mulroney said ... the native deal created no new land rights, a big concern in Quebec, where Cree Indian and Inuit Eskimo groups claim large tracts. – *The Independent*, 22 August 1982.

Insistence (by others) that 'eskimo' be abandoned may just have something to do with the fact that 'Eskimo Pie' was the name given (in the US, from 1921) to an ice-cream bar covered with chocolate.

intellectually challenged: See -CHALLENGED.

[invalid]: 'The word "invalid" suggests someone who is "not valid" ' – Briefing Note, The Royal Association for Disability and Rehabilitation, May 1992.

Besides, a disabled person may not be ill. Disability should not be confused with illness.

involuntarily leisured: To be used instead of **[unemployed]**.

[IRISH JOKES]: Like [ESSEX GIRL JOKES], these are definitely not PC. Popular since the 1970s, they are based on the popular belief that Irish people are intellectually challenged (see -CHALLENGED). For example, there was the instruction that had to be given to the Irish gardener laying turf – 'Green side *up*, Paddy, green side *up!*' On the other hand, the Irish are very good themselves at producing Irish jokes (though sometimes these take the form of English jokes, e.g. 'How do you save an Englishman from drowning?' 'I don't know.' 'Good.'). They also have what are called Kerry jokes – exactly the same kind of shafts, aimed at the rustic residents of County Kerry. In fact, most nationalities seem to have these jokes about other nationalities, or about sub-groups within themselves. Americans have Polish jokes about [POLACKS]. Texans poke fun at East Texans. In South Africa, van der Moerwe jokes mock the sluggish Afrikaans mentality. Jewish jokes are known worldwide and told by Jewish people as much as, if not more so, than by other people.

Even so, wherever they arise, such jokes are a serious crime as far as the INAPPROPRIATELY DIRECTED LAUGHTER police is concerned.

islanders: See [NATIVES].

-ISM: This suffix has almost become a pejorative term in its own right: one often sees references to 'isms' as being a bad thing. At one time, this meant the political '-isms' of Communism, Fascism, Marxism, Socialism, but now could be used about all the politically correct or incorrect '-isms'. These may be divided conveniently into positive and negative '-isms'.

For positive '-isms' see: AFROCENTRISM, ANIMALISM, FEMINISM, GENDERISM, MULTICULTURALISM, WOMANISM.

For negative '-isms' see: ABLEISM/ABLISM (and able-bodism, able-bodiedism), AGEISM/AGISM, ALPHABETISM, ANIMALISM (second meaning), DISABLISM, DISEASEISM, EUROCENTRISM, FAT(TY)ISM, HAIRISM, HANDICAPPISM, HANDISM, HEIGHTISM, HETEROSEXISM, HUEISM, LOOKISM, MASCUL(IN)ISM, PHALLOCENTRICISM, RACISM, SCENTISM, SEXISM, SIGHTISM, SIZISM, SMELLISM, SMOKEISM, SPECISM/SPECIESISM, TOKENISM, UGLYISM, UNCLE TOMISM, WEIGHTISM.

The mostly nonce-coinages include FAT(TY)ISM, HANDICAPPISM, HUEISM, MASCUL(IN)ISM, SMOKEISM.

-IST: A janus suffix denoting opposites: either (a) one who behaves in a disapproved of fashion (AGEIST, CLASSIST, HETEROSEXIST, HOMOSEXUALIST, MASCULIST/MASCULINIST, SEXIST, RACIST) derogatory) or (b) one who supports or is concerned with a certain cause (ANIMALIST, FEMINIST) (non-derogatory).

Many of the resulting '-ist' words are nonce-coinages. For example, 'Do you feel that there is something unacceptably **MINERALIST** about the strictures on lead voiced by a lady called Silbergeld?' – *The Economist*, 1 April 1989.

Italian/Italian-American: See [EYETIE].

[Iti/Ity]: See [EYETIE].

J

janitor: See [CHARWOMAN].

[Jap]/Japanese: See [NIP].

Jewish: What is the PC way of referring to a **Jew**? This has been a question fraught with difficulties not just for years but for centuries. The word 'Hebrew' was used in the nineteenth century to make clear that the word 'Jew' was not being used in its derogatory sense of usurer, moneylender or extortionate tradesman. Sobriquets like 'The Chosen People' (self-applied, from the Old Testament) and 'The People of the Book' (as they are called by Muslims) were other euphemisms, but are not appropriate here. **Jewish person** is probably the safest all-round term. Jonathan Miller pointed the way in a groundbreaking *Beyond the Fringe* sketch in 1961. When Alan Bennett pointed out that Miller was 'a Jew', he replied by saying that, rather, he was 'not really a Jew, but Jew*ish* – not the whole hog'.

Nevertheless, *The Oxford English Dictionary* (Second Edition) continues to carry the definition of 'Jewish' as 'chiefly referring to the extortion or overreaching attributed to Jewish money-lenders'. Labelled 'offensive', this meaning continues to upset Jewish people and, though a historical fact, its mere inclusion in the dictionary has frequently been challenged. Should dictionaries include and thus perpetuate offensive usage? In 1973, a merchant claimed that the definitions of 'Jew' in the Oxford Dictionaries were 'scurrilous and defamatory'. The case was lost on a question of law, not fact (see *The Times*, 6 July 1973).

All derogatory terms for Jewish people are naturally non-PC. This includes words like **[jewboy]** and **[yid]** which were commonly used in the early part of this century before sensitivities were heightened by the Holocaust. **[Ike, ikey, iky, ikeymo]** are all derogatory terms derived from the name Isaac and are, similarly, now held to be totally offensive. Charles Dickens, who subsequently offended Jewish sensibilities with the character of Fagin in *Oliver Twist*, (1837), but redeemed himself with Mr Riah in *Our Mutual Friend*, (1864), used the word 'Ikey' in *Sketches by Boz* (1835).

[Kike] is an offensive, mostly US term, and is thought to be a variant of *kiki*, a duplication of the common *-ki* ending of the names of many Jews from Slav countries. Leo Rosten, however, in *The Joys of Yiddish* (1968) suggests that the word comes from Ellis Island immigration officers who, faced with Jewish immigrants unable to write their names in the Roman alphabet, instructed them to sign their names with a cross. For understandable reasons, they chose to put instead a circle as a means of identification. For the Jews, a circle (Yiddish, *kikel*) is a symbol of unending life. To the immigration officers, a person who asked to be allowed to make a *kikel* or a *kikeleh* (a little circle) soon became a 'kikee' or simply a 'kike'.

See also -CHALLENGED.

[jokestress]: I can't believe that this term for a female comedian – in fact, the full phrase used in *Cosmopolitan* (UK), February 1987, was the tautological 'female jokestress' – can be politically correct. Presumably the intention was to ring the changes on the word 'comedian' without resorting to **[comedienne]**. If there is a PC word for this kind of person, I haven't encountered it yet, though 'comedy person' or simply 'entertainer' ought to do.

[jungle]: This word is unacceptable these days, because of derogatory associations with the 'law of the jungle', 'The Blackboard Jungle', 'The Asphalt Jungle', 'just down from the trees', etc. Tarzan now has to hack his way through the **tropical rain forest** which, alas, just isn't quite the same somehow.

K

[Kaffir/kaffir]: The white southern African derogatory term for a black man has long been seen as offensive – even by those inclined to use it. The word appears to derive from the Arab word for 'infidel', as applied to all non-Muslims.

> How, for instance, does one describe negroid South Africans? The early missionary word 'kaffir' meaning heathen, has become a term of abuse. – *The New Statesman*, 2 May 1959.

> A mob which swore at the police, called them 'white Kaffirs', and hurled bottles at them. – *The Cape Times*, 6 September 1960.

> Kaffir is the term used by Europeans to describe all black people in Africa irrespective of their race and origin. – Laurens van der Post, *The Heart of the Hunter* (1961).

> When we ... were young people the word 'kaffir' meant nothing more than to indicate a Black man ... It has deteriorated to such an extent that it offends people with a dark coloured skin and ... we try to avoid it. – *Debates of the Senate of South Africa*, 17 May 1973.

By the 1940s this awareness of the offence-giving power of the word appears to have led to the coining of the alternative word **[Fanagolo]** in the South African mining community. This possibly derives from *kuluma fana ga lo* meaning 'to speak like this' which, if true, is a curious parallel with the derivation of [SPIC] from 'speaka da English'.

But the newer coinage is still unacceptable. Whether the dismantling of apartheid will lead to the complete disappearance of official terms such as 'Cape Coloured' – the name given to the 'coloured or brown population' of Cape Province – remains to be seen. Will a PC term for a South African black person emerge along the lines of AFRICAN-AMERICAN and PERSON OF COLO(U)R?

(*Sources include: The Oxford English Dictionary*, Second Edition.)

[kept woman]: See [MISTRESS].

[kike]: See JEWISH.

[knacker]: The terms **meat dealer** and **meat man** have been heard but the activity is probably so un-PC that no word could possibly be found to describe it.

Kwanzaa: An 'African-American Yule-time Celebration' i.e. not **[Christmas].** 'Three years ago, the Smithsonian in Washington added "Kwanzaa" (a complete invention by a black-studies professor at California State University) to Hanukkah and Christmas exhibitions'. – *The Observer*, 29 December 1991.

L

[lady/ladies]: 'Women is usually better as in the Women's Singles Final. Phrases like dinner ladies and cleaning ladies come across as condescending. Cooks, catering staff and cleaners are perfectly adequate.' – 'Guidelines for Factual Programmes', BBC (1989).

larger than average: See [FAT].

[later years, the]: See THIRD AGE.

LBG: See GAY.

learning difficulties: See [MENTALLY HANDICAPPED].

learning disabled: See [MENTALLY HANDICAPPED].

learning disorders: See [MENTALLY HANDICAPPED].

lesbian: See GAY.

[lie]: See COUNTER-FACTUAL PROPOSITION.

[linguistically challenged]: See -CHALLENGED.

[little lady]: Avoid – according to Rosalie Maggio, *The Nonsexist Word Finder: A Dictionary of Gender-Free Usage*, Boston, Mass., (1988): 'The very intent is demeaning. It is also incorrect to refer to a child this way because (1) a child is not an adult and should be allowed to be a child while she is a child and (2) telling a child she is a little lady almost without exception is an attempt to perpetuate some cultural stereotype e.g. sitting quietly and neatly in the background.'

An example: 'Now, now little lady, you don't want to believe all those things you read in the newspapers about crisis and upheavals, and the end of civilization as we know it. Dearie me, not at all.' (*The Daily Telegraph*, 10 June 1976.) This was a *parody* of James Callaghan's style, when Prime Minister, of addressing Margaret Thatcher. Written by John O'Sullivan, it was quoted in all seriousness by *Time* magazine.

See also [DEAR], [GIRL(S)] and [LOVE].

lone parent: See [SINGLE PARENT].

longer living, the: See [OLD].

LOOKISM/LOOKSISM: Discrimination or prejudice against other people on the grounds of their (usually) unpleasant looks (compare UGLYISM). Presumably, the reason for 'lookism' surviving whereas 'looksism' has not is because the latter, original form is virtually impossible to say.

Looksism gives birth to fatism, another cruel stereotype that affects us all. – Rita Freedman, *Bodylove* (1988).

A Smith College handout from the Office of Student Affairs lists 10 different kinds of oppression that can be inflicted by making judgements about people . . . 'lookism . . . construction of a standard for beauty/attractiveness'. It's not sufficient to avoid discriminating against unattractive people; you must suppress the impulse to notice the difference. – Jerry Ardler *et al.*, 'Thought Police', *Newsweek*, 14 January 1991.

The forces of political correctness probably have long since banished much retrograde language. ('Purdue has men who dare and do, and comely co-eds too.' To call a young woman a co-ed is sexism; to call her comely is 'lookism'.) – *The Washington Post*, 24 October 1991.

Compare also ANIMAL LOOKISM.

[loony bin]: As with **[lunatic asylum]** and **[madhouse],** this is an expression that still has a certain self-conscious currency even, or especially, among those who administer such places. 'Lunatic asylum' was, however, considered politically correct in the early nineteenth century when it took over from the previous century's 'lunatic hospital/house' and, especially, was preferred to the seventeenth century term 'madhouse'.

The earliest citation to hand for 'loony bin ... the facetious term for a mental hospital' in *The Oxford English Dictionary* (Second Edition) is from *My Man Jeeves* (1919) by P.G. Wodehouse.

Elsewhere, euphemisms rule. **Mental home** and **mental institution** are still reasonably PC usage, though both frequently undergo a further euphemistic layer when used in such statements as, 'Oh, He's in a home', 'he's in an institution', or even, 'He's had to be sent away.'

See also MAD.

(*Sources include:* Vernon Noble, *Speak Softly – Euphemisms and Such*, 1982.)

[looter]: See NON-TRADITIONAL SHOPPER.

[love]: Indiscriminate sprinkling of this albeit token endearment whether by bus conductors (at the end of every sentence) or actors (at the end of every phrase) is not approved. The very-PC Glenys Kinnock made specific mention of her husband Neil's predilection for this incorrect word, when he was Leader of Britain's Labour Party. It is believed however that the word may be exchanged between consenting adults in private. Compare [DEAR] and [LITTLE LADY].

lover: Like **partner** this is a PC term that may refer to a mistress, girlfriend, wife, boyfriend, homosexual paramour, or husband. The term's correctness presumably lies, thus, in its imprecision – and lack of usefulness.

lower income bracket, those in the: See [POOR].

[lunatic asylum]: See [LOONY BIN].

M

mad: Most of the euphemisms are unacceptable: **[mental, mentally deranged/disordered/disturbed, suffering from a mental condition/mental alienation, unbalanced].** The PC oracle has not come up with anything better, and so it is quite in order to call mad people 'mad'. If they do not consider this politically correct, they will probably point this out to you, forcibly. See also [LOONY BIN].

[madhouse]: See [LOONY BIN].

[maiden name]: A totally unacceptable concept, implying as it does that all unmarried women are virgins (which is probably not the case). Substitute **family name** or **birth name.**

(*Sources include:* Val Dumond, *The Elements of Nonsexist Usage*, New York, 1990; *The Sunday Telegraph*, 8 March 1992.)

[majorette]: See [-ETTE SUFFIX].

male fantasy: A term for any MASCULIST behaviour that offends against the canons of feminist good taste.

Male fantasy of lonely chick masturbating in sad need of him. – Kate Millett, *Flying* (1974).

No amount of simulated cunnilingus can make them any more than a male fantasy, with Stone orgasming the minute she mounts Douglas [in the film *Basic Instinct*]. It's the familiar 'Look Ma! No hands' approach and deeply dissatisfying. – *The Guardian*, 7 May 1992.

[man]: This term is only PC when it refers to an adult male human, and should not really be used even then. The *New York Times* style book demands ADULT MALE for 'man', according to *The Independent* (21 July 1992).

Whatever the case, the word should never be used as inclusive of all humans. An early offender here, in more ways than one, was G.K. Chesterton, who wrote: 'Individually, men may present a more or less rational appearance, eating, sleeping and scheming. But humanity as a whole is changeful, mystical, fickle and delightful. Men are men, but Man is a woman.' – *The Napoleon of Notting Hill* (1904).

To include women in a word like *man* or *mankind* suggests that they don't merit their own word, that they must be content to be included in the generic *man*. Women become conditioned to borrowing men's descriptions . . . work . . . and even men's ideas. The result of this emphasis on men's contributions to civilization is the repetitious message that women are also-rans, second-class citizens, tag-alongs, things. – Val Dumond, *The Elements of Nonsexist Usage*, New York, 1990.

Those resisting language reform often say that the meaning of *man* is clear: context alone allows us to distinguish between its sex-specific and its generic use. However, since the early 1970s, researchers have studied what children, high school students, and adults understand when they encounter the term *man*. Studies summarized by Wendy Martyna (1978) show that, in response to the generic *man* and *he*, women, men and children alike form mental pictures of males, thus seriously undermining the efficiency of *man* and *he* as generic terms. Further, we encounter intended sex-specific usage far more often than generic usage. – Ruth King (ed.), *Talking Gender: A Guide to Nonsexist Communication*, Toronto, 1991.

'Guidelines for Factual Programmes', BBC (1989), states of 'Men': 'Usually better as "people", "staff", "workforce", "workers", "union members", "trade unionists", "employees" or a "factory employing 3,000".'

[manhole]: See FEMHOLE.

[mankind]: For the reasons rehearsed under [MAN], substitute **humankind**.

> Columnists hoot at news of students boycotting the classics, insisting on 'humankind' rather than 'mankind'. *The Washington Post*, 3 February 1991.

[manning]: See STAFFING.

MASCULINISM/MASCULISM: The promotion or continuance of a dominant role for men in any society. The concept has enjoyed a renaissance since about 1988, though Virginia Woolf had used 'masculinism' to describe exactly the same thing as long ago as 1918. See -ISM, and the following entry.

MASCULIST/MASCULINIST: A person who asserts the superiority of men over women. Compare FEMINIST – which is the advocacy of women's rights, not usually their superiority or dominance. 'Masculist' was coined in the US in the early 1980s. The earlier form 'masculinist' was current by 1918.

> What is claimed to be the first ever European petition for men's rights is to be handed in to the European Parliament by a new 'masculist' group . . . There are already some 20,000 militant masculists in Europe. – *The Times*, 20 March 1984.

> Another recent victory is for Anglican feminists: masculist language is to go from Church of England services. Mankind shall be no more . . . [but] God is to remain male at least for the time being. – *Sunday Telegraph*, 16 July 1989.

(*Sources include: The Longman Register of New Words*, 1990.)

[mastery] PC alternatives include: 'proficiency, understanding, knowledge, accomplishment, acquaintance with, competency, excellence, facility, advantage, adeptness, skill, dexterity, deftness, expertise, rule, victory, ascendency, supremacy, authority, subjugation, conquest, control, domination, upper hand, reins in one's hands, commands, order, sway'. This thesaurus-full is from Rosalie Maggio, *The Nonsexist Word Finder: A Dictionary of Gender-Free Usage*, Boston, Mass., (1988).

See also the Introduction.

[mature travellers]: See [OLD].

[mature woman]: See [MIDDLE-AGED WOMAN].

meat dealer/man: See [KNACKER].

[meat-eating]: The concept is so repulsive (not to say ANIMALIST) that only the term **non-vegetarian** will do. Actually, a joke-coinage:

> There was a box-office jackpot for *Robin Hood Prince of Thieves*, whose hero knocked off more Normans in his time than Hannibal Lecter had non-vegetarian dinners. – *The Financial Times*, 2 January 1992.

meat-purveyor: See [BUTCHER].

[menopause]: What on earth is 'men' doing in there? 'Male menopause' sounds like a tautology. How odd that there doesn't appear to be a PC term for this – though perhaps 'gynaecologically challenged' (see -CHALLENGED) could be brought into play here also. ' "Menopause" is a neutral term describing a physical reality that is very different for different women; avoid stereotyping it.' – Rosalie Maggio, *The Nonsexist Word Finder: A Dictionary of Gender-Free Usage*, Boston, Mass., (1988).

[menstruate]: See FEMSTRUATE.

[menstruating]: See -CHALLENGED.

[mental age of –, has a]: See [MENTALLY HANDICAPPED].

mental home/institution: See [LOONY BIN]

[mentally deficient]: See [MENTALLY HANDICAPPED].

[mentally deranged, etc.] See MAD.

[mentally handicapped]: Various attempts have been made over the years to find a way round this descriptive but slightly brutal phrase (which was current by 1919). It is obviously an improvement upon such older terms as **[backward]**, **[mentally deficient]**, and **[retarded]**. The vaguer **[subnormal]** was current in its own right in 1919; as **[educationally subnormal]** – a term applied to mentally backward children who could not be taught in ordinary schools – by 1953 (and abbreviated to 'E.S.N.' by 1960).

More euphemistic terms have proliferated in recent years, like **[with learning disorders]**, for example.

Young children with learning disorders are less likely to have been breast-fed than children who do not have these disorders, according to a paediatrician. – *The Sunday Times*, 17 April 1977.

Slow learner was being used loosely by 1981, though some restricted its use to people who were E.S.N. Again, the phrases were being used to cover a wide variety of states and conditions, not always comparable. Fven more recently, we have had attempts to use such positive words as **exceptional** and **special** to describe people in this field, but, like the phrase **with special needs**, in general medical terminology, these terms are loose or vague to the extent of pointlessness.

Adopting Children with Special Needs. – Title of book edited by Joan McNamara (1975).

Yes, there is a meeting *tonight* at one of the area high schools for people interested in being parents for special needs children. – Claudia L. Jewett, *Adopting the Older Child*, Boston, Mass., 1978.

Then along came **people with learning difficulties**. As a sub-stitute phrase for 'mentally handicapped', this term is rejected by the charity, Mencap, which after all has an interest in retaining the well-established phrase alluded to in its name. In July 1992, the charity said the new phrase was 'inaccurate' and that using it in answer to demands from charity and social workers would cost Mencap support because the public 'would not understand it'.

Steven Billington, Mencap's director of marketing and appeals, said, 'It is only a matter of time before even the most right-on expression becomes a term of abuse. It has been the same since people talked about village idiots, and "learning difficulties" is no exception. Children are already calling each other LDs as an insult.' Lord Rix, Mencap's chairman, said: ' "learning difficulties" is a misnomer. It implies that mental handicap is all a matter of educa-tion ... My child [born mentally handicapped] is 40 and to describe her as having a learning difficulty is a travesty of the truth.' (*The Independent*, 20 July 1992.)

People with learning disabilities is another of the alternatives on offer but sounds like a compromise and is unlikely to gain wide-spread acceptance. It has however been used by Mencap in some of its campaigns. Mencap was founded principally as a parents' organization. Lobbies such as one called People First demand that the choice of nomenclature should be decided by the people who actually have the disabilities. Some of these would support the new terms, some the old, and some, of course, would not be capable of offering an opinion.

In cautioning against putting too much emphasis on early French immersion for the majority of children, the report says such programs may harm children with learning difficulties. – *The Globe and Mail* (Toronto), 25 August 1976.

When I heard that someone had 'learning difficulties', I had no idea what it meant ... If someone has learning difficulties, it could be because their school was burnt down, because they are deaf, because they are in the Tory Cabinet, because all their teachers are talking a foreign language or many other reasons, one of which might be a physical or psychological inability to learn. – *The Independent*, 20 January 1992.

Learning-disabled might appear to be a fraction more precise but still contains the disputed 'learning' qualification.

Sean, 20, is learning-disabled, and his co-workers are afflicted with manic depression, deafness, schizophrenia and other disabilities. – *People Weekly*, 10 October 1988.

So what is to be done?

There is growing dissatisfaction with the term 'mental handicap' because it tends to be used as a blanket definition and because it has so many negative connotations. It is inadequate as a definition because of the enormous range of mental impairment it has to cover ... 'Learning difficulties' has in turn been criticised for being imprecise and for being even more open to misinterpretation than 'mental handicap' ... One strategy may be to use both terms together: 'learning difficulties, formerly known as mental handicap'. – 'Guide to the Representation of People With Disabilities in Programmes', compiled by Geoffrey Prout, BBC, 1990.

This dual-use compromise apparently operated in this newspaper feature:

[Flat, a voluntary organization] has two registered care homes where mentally handicapped people live for a short time to learn such skills as shopping, cooking and budgeting . . . [*Picture caption:*] A cookery class in Peckham, south London, where patients with learning difficulties can tackle pizza, shepherd's pie and other dishes with the help of pictorial recipes. – *The Independent*, 23 May 1992.

It should hardly be necessary to say that the following words should never be used now in this context: **[cretin]**, **[defective]**, [freak], [imbecile], [paralytic], and [vegetable]. [Has a mental age of –] is considered unnecessarily harsh. Substitute 'has a severe mental handicap/learning difficulties'.

See also [-HANDICAPPED/THE HANDICAPPED].

(*Sources include:* Vernon Noble, *Speak Softly – Euphemisms and Such*, 1982.)

metabolically challenged: See -CHALLENGED.

[Mexican-American]: See CHICANA/CHICANO.

[middle-aged woman]: An equivalent of the French expression *'une femme d'une certaine âge'* ('a woman of a certain age') has never caught on in English. A phrase like **[mature woman]** – as in 'fashions for the mature woman' – would certainly not do. It might suggest that the woman was once immature.

[midget]: See PERSON OF RESTRICTED GROWTH.

MINERALIST: See -IST.

minorities: Given that these are the *raison d'être* of political correctness, it is worth pointing out that they should really be thought of in a more positive light. They are 'part of the world's majorities' – at least, according to the report 'One Nation; Many Peoples: a Declaration of Cultural Independence' issued by the New York State Board of Education (1991).

(*Source: The Independent*, 8 July 1991.)

[miss]: See MS.

[mistress]: Val Dumond, in *The Elements of Nonsexist Usage* (New York, 1990), instructs that this term be eliminated 'unless there is an equal term for men in the same position'. Well, is there? LOVER is hardly descriptive enough.

[Kept woman] is similarly unacceptable.

[mongolism]: See DOWN'S SYNDROME.

morally challenged: See -CHALLENGED.

morally different: See [DISHONEST].

[Mrs]: See MS.

Ms.: 'Ms' (pronounced *miz*) is 'a title substituted for **[Mrs]** or **[Miss]** before a woman's name to avoid making a distinction between married and unmarried women', according to the *Collins Dictionary of the English Language* (1979). Thus, it is a compromise (between 'Mrs' and 'Miss'), designed to solve a problem, and sounding every bit like the compromise it is.

'Ms' became popular with feminists in about 1970 at the start of the modern thrust by the Women's Movement. The New York Commission on Human Rights adopted it for use in correspondence at about that time. By 1972, a feminist magazine called *Ms* was launched.

The idea had been around for some time before it became – in the words of the *Oxford English Dictionary* (Second Edition) – 'an increasingly common, but not universally accepted, use'. This, from the early 1950s:

> Use the abbreviation Ms for *all women* addressees. This modern style solves an age-old problem. – *The Simplified Letter*, issued by the National Office Management Association, Philadelphia, 4 January 1952.

But it created a new problem. In August 1984, Geraldine Ferraro was the first woman to be selected as an American vice-presidential candidate. In what is known as 'private life', she was, in fact, Mrs John Zaccaro. In public she declined to be known as 'Miss Ferraro', feeling this was inapposite for a woman who was the mother of three children. She asked that she be called either 'Ms' or 'Mrs' Ferraro.

The *New York Times* in its traditional way, found this very hard to swallow. The paper liked to attach honorifics to names but did not permit the use of 'Ms' in its columns and had to call her 'Mrs

Ferraro' – despite pleadings from its own word expert, William Safire, who protested that 'Mrs Ferraro' is 'a person she is not ... It is unacceptable for journalists to dictate to a candidate that she call herself Miss or else use her married name.' In 1986, the newspaper gave way. But one can understand its reluctance to accept 'Ms' – not for opposing the motives behind its creation, but because it is not an elegant coinage. Many people seem quite happy to use it, nevertheless.

(*Sources include: Time*, 20 August 1984; Nigel Rees, *Why Do We Say ... ?*, 1987; Nigel Rees, *Best Behaviour*, 1992.)

MULTICULTURALISM: The driving force behind PC in the US. It stands for the proliferation of 'differences', as opposed to adherence to one main (white, European) culture, and accordingly embraces and champions all minorities.

Most of those who tolerate or even advocate multiculturalism in our schools and colleges have educational, not ideological, intentions. But the force is with the extremists who ride roughshod over the opposition by intimidating it with accusations of 'racism'. – Irving Kristol, *The New York Times*, 31 July 1991.

Christina Hoff Sommers, a philosophy professor at Clark University in Worcester, Mass., criticized ... as 'somewhat intrusive' a Clark survey that asked professors 'how they intended to incorporate diversity and multiculturalism into the classes'. – *The Washington Post*, 31 October 1991.

The word 'multicultural' was known by 1941 in the US; 'multi-culturalism' by 1965, especially in Canada.

[murderer]: See OFFENDER.

N

Native Alaskan: See INNUIT.

Native American: See [RED INDIAN].

[natives]: Quite unacceptable. Hence, Robinson Crusoe now has to tangle with **islanders** or **indigenous peoples**.

> [In] one of three stories shortlisted for [Terry] Jones to read on Jackanory in November ... 'I wrote that the sailor landed and met a native. The fax came whirring back at me, complaining about the word native. All it means, of course, is that he met a man who lives there. But I had to change it to "a man with a spear".' He sighs. – *The Evening Standard* (London), 5 October 1992.

negative images: See POSITIVE IMAGES.

NEUTRALIZATION, SEXUAL: See -PERSON.

[newsmen]: 'Instead say journalists, reporters, media representatives, TV crews (depending on context)' – 'Guidelines for Factual Programmes', BBC (1989).

[nigger]: The removal of this word for 'a Negro' from English language use was the most notable achievement of pre-PC language policing. *The Oxford English Dictionary* (Second Edition) neatly explains: 'Except in Black English vernacular,where it remains common, [it is] now virtually restricted to contexts of deliberate and contemptuous verbal abuse.' Hence, nowadays, the only acceptable use of the word is by the minority so described (compare 'bent', DYKE and 'queer' in homosexual usage).

According to Stuart Berg Flexner in *I Hear America Talking* (1976), 'nigger' originated as a 'northern England (and Irish) dialect pronunciation of Negro, being first recorded in English as *neger* in 1587. When the very first slaves were brought to the American colonies in 1619, John Rolfe of Jamestown, Virginia wrote in his *Journal*, "A Dutch ship sold us twenty Negars . . .".'

It is difficult to say precisely when the word 'nigger' began to be considered so utterly repellent. Flexner suggests about 1825, 'when both abolitionists and Blacks began to object to it as disparaging. Then after the Civil War *nigger* became the most common contemptuous word for a Black.' In our own century, I would suggest that white Americans began to be genuinely embarrassed about it in the 1950s, though by 1949 it was being noted that, 'Negro has taken over the objectionable word "nigger" (though not "darky") and made it a test of praise or blame.' (B.A. Botkin, ed., *A Treasury of Southern Folklore*.)

In 1950s Britain, too, I recall registering that Agatha Christie's novel *Ten Little Niggers* was known in the US as *Ten Little Indians*. This was not entirely a matter of sensitivity, however. Christie's novel had been published in 1939 but re-titled for the American edition. *And Then There Were None* was the original title of the US 1945 film (known in the UK, however, as *Ten Little Niggers*). The UK 1966 film *Ten Little Niggers* was called *Ten Little Indians* in the US. The UK 1974 film was known in the US and UK as *And Then There Were None*.

In fact, though, the song alluded to by Agatha Christie in her book (and play) was actually 'Ten Little Injuns' all along. *That* was the title of the *original* song, written by the US songwriter Septimus Winner (*c* 1868). Frank Green's British version, 'Ten Little Niggers' was published in 1869, and is the one that begins:

Ten little nigger boys went out to dine;
One choked his little self, and then there were nine.

Despite these diversions, in the United States, 'negro' – at some time in the mid-twentieth century – became the accepted term.

Then **colo(u)red** came into favour again, as in the name of the National Association for the Advancement of Colored People (a title that is still used). As Stuart Berg Flexner charts it, however, '*black* dates from the earliest days of slavery and was more common than *negro* until the Civil War. Since *black* was considered a slave term Blacks preferred to be called *colored* from after the war until the late 1880s; from the late 1880s until the 1930s they preferred to be called *negroes* (with a capital *N* after the late 1920s).'

In the 1960s, **black** or **Black** came so much to the fore that it seemed no other term would ever be needed. It was used in such slogans as 'Black Power' and 'Black is beautiful'. The former encompassed just about anything that people wanted it to mean, from simple pride in the black race to a threat of violence. Adam Clayton Powell Jr, the Harlem congressman, said in a baccalaureate address at Howard University in May 1966: 'To demand these God-given rights is to seek black power – what I call audacious power – the power to build black institutions of splendid achievement.' On 6 June the same year, James Meredith, the first black to integrate the University of Mississippi (in 1962), was shot and wounded during a civil rights march. Stokely Carmichael, heading the Student Non-violent Coordinating Committee, continued the march, during which his contingent first used the phrase as a shout. In the same month, Carmichael used the phrase in a speech at Greenwood, Mississippi. It was also adopted as a slogan by the Congress for Racial Equality. However, the notion was not new in the 1960s. Langston Hughes had written in *Simple Takes a Wife* (1953): 'Negro blood is so powerful – because just *one* drop of black blood makes a coloured man – *one* drop – you are a Negro! ... Black is powerful.' The Revd Dr Martin Luther King Jr launched a poster campaign based on 'Black is beautiful' in 1967, but Stokely Carmichael had used the phrase at a Memphis civil rights rally in 1966. It may have its origins in the Song of Solomon 1:5: 'I am black, but comely.'

But 'black/Black' has apparently had its day. We have had AFRO-AMERICAN, in its place, and now AFRICAN-AMERICAN. One must not forget, of course, 'negro/Negro' inclusion among the PEOPLE OF COLO(U)R.

UK usage has bumped along in the wake of US custom in recent decades. Jennifer Wayne in her reminiscences *The Purple Dress* (1979), about her broadcasting work in the Second World War, notes: 'The BBC had a formidable list of forbidden words or expressions: "nigger" was banned; so was "black"; you had to say "coloured".'

And 'coloured' it remained – also for African and Asian immigrants to Britain – until the change of heart spear-headed by the switch to 'black', in the US, during the 1960s. Yet even in 1976 (4 May), *The Guardian* was still writing this: 'The children of coloured immigrants are commonly regarded as being at the bottom of the heap as far as educational achievement and job prospects are concerned.'

In the same paper a black reporter wrote about his experiences when interviewing people: 'There is always that little pause while they decide whether to be direct and say black or use the euphemistic coloured. And, typically, they can never decide . . .'

(*Sources include:* Vernon Noble, *Speak Softly – Euphemisms and Such*, 1982; Nigel Rees, *Dictionary of Phrase & Allusion*, 1991.)

[Nip]: Does anybody use this offensive term these days for a Japanese? Derived from *Nippon*, the Japanese name for Japan (literally, 'the land of the rising sun'), the word had its heyday in the early 1940s. Now one would be more likely to hear the comparatively mild **[Jap]** used abusively. **Japanese** is the only PC word.

non-aboriginal Australians: See ABORIGINAL/ABORIGINE.

non-human animal: What was formerly known as just an animal. This preferred term puts humans in their place and reminds them that they are no better than they are.

non-human animal companion: See ANIMAL COMPANION.

NON-JUDGEMENTAL: The prime aim of politically correct coinages is to be this.

non-vegetarian: See [MEAT-EATING].

NON-SEXIST LANGUAGE: Val Dumond in *The Elements of Non-sexist Usage* (New York, 1990), writes: 'Over the past 20 years, several contrived words have been offered to solve the problem of sexism in language. Most of these offerings are what they appear to be – contrived to cover a gap in the English language. They include *she/he, (s)he, co, cos, sher, shim, herm, heris, tey, tem, ter(s), ve, ver* ... and the list goes on. However, it isn't mecessary to go to these lengths in order to eliminate or at least reduce sexism in today's language [though] the need to make an attempt is increasing.'

  She goes on: '[Non-sexist] terminology is used to label the kind of language that refuses to discriminate according to gender. It is invariably called *nonsexist, genderless, gender-free, gender-neutral, inclusive, nonbiased,* or *unbiased language.*'

non-traditional shopper: A joke term for **[looter]** – from *The New York Times*, July 1992.

North American Indian: See [RED INDIAN].

[not so slim as one would like to be]: See [FAT].

nutritional shortfall: See [HUNGER].

O

[O.A.P.]: See [OLD].

[obese]: See [FAT].

offender: Always to be used in preference to **[burglar]**, **[criminal]** or **[murderer]**. A more sensitive and NON-JUDGEMENTAL usage.

(*Source: The Sunday Telegraph*, 8 March 1992.)

office cleaning operative: See [CLEANING LADY].

[old]: 'Old age' is a concept so unspeakable that euphemisms have been queuing up for years to take its place. 'Getting on (in years)', 'not as young as he/she used to be', 'venerable' are but three of the, er, venerable, traditional euphemisms on this score. Advertising holidays for the 'Over 60s' is another common way round the problem. One such advert, in the *Radio Times* (February 1981), said it contained information for **[mature travellers]** – but this can be objected to on the same grounds as 'mature woman' (see [MIDDLE-AGED WOMAN]). *The Times*, 22 January 1992, had **age-ful**, which is so inappropriate, it almost hurts.

Equally offensive, it appears, is any reference to **[the elderly]**:

It is extremely disheartening that you should be so ageist as to head the article 'Care of the Elderly'. 'The elderly' is a figure of speech, metonymy, in which one attribute is used to describe the whole, just as in 'the Irish', 'the blacks' ... and 'the delinquents'. – Letter to *The Lancet*, 19 August 1978.

For many years, the term **[O.A.P.]** was in official use, originally meaning 'Old Age Pension' (by 1942), and then 'Old Age Pensioner'. But the Sensitivity Police eventually sank it, presumably on the grounds that each of the three component words was somehow objectionable. **Senior Citizen** was imported from the US in about 1938 and has had a certain success because of its alliteration but still sounds a touch patronizing. **[Veteran]** would not do because of its military connotations. **Golden-ager**, which was current in the US by 1961, seems never to have weathered the trip across the Atlantic. Nor has the American term **the longer living.**

Consider also **chronologically gifted/challenged** and **experientially enhanced** – all joke coinages from the US. **Seasoned** does not seem likely to catch on – for largely culinary reasons.

See also -CHALLENGED and THIRD AGE.

(*Sources include: The Oxford English Dictionary* (Second Edition); Vernon Noble, *Speak Softly – Euphemisms and Such*, 1982.)

[old maid]: See [SPINSTER].

-operative: As in RODENT OPERATIVE, this is a euphemism for '(skilled) worker' and is all part of the job enhancement process. For some reason, it was not deemed suitable when the term SEX WORKER came to be coined.

oppressive attitudes: What PCPs seek to reveal through AWARENESS EXERCISES.

oppressor: A person who is the target of most PC field work. He is, naturally, for the most part a white heterosexual adult male human.

Some of the jokes, in truth, are good: a politically correct revival of *Guys and Dolls* is to be called 'Loathsome Oppressors and Women of Vision and Strength'. – *The Washington Post*, 3 February 1992.

In British Labour Party circles, BBC Radio's agricultural soap opera *The Archers* is known, jokingly, as *The Grundys and Their Oppressors*.

optically challenged: See [BLIND] and -CHALLENGED.

[Oriental]: See ASIAN-AMERICAN.

[orphan]: See PARENTALLY DISADVANTAGED.

otherly abled/otherwise abled: See -ABLED and DISABLED.

orthographically challenged: Used of Vice-President J. Danforth Quayle's inability to spell 'potato' without an 'e' – *The Guardian* (1992). See -CHALLENGED.

[outsize(d)]: See [FAT].

[over-shapely]: See [FAT].

P

[paleface]: This old [RED INDIAN] term for a white man (established by the 1820s) appears now to be non-PC, if a dispute over its use in a Coppertone sun-tan lotion advertising sign in Miami is anything to go by. For many years Coppertone used a picture of a little girl having her bathing suit being pulled down by a spaniel, coupled with the slogans 'Tan – don't burn' and 'Don't be a paleface!'

> The billboard's pro-tan message in the era of thinning ozone layers is no longer consistent with Coppertone's new emphasis on sunscreens. And, a company spokesman conceded, 'different sensitivities' make it unwise to push a slogan containing the politicially incorrect word 'paleface'. – *The Economist*, 14 September 1991.

> A group of Dubuque citizens launched an enterprise – 'constructive integration' – to bring one hundred black families to the city over the next few years. This initiative angered some people of paleface, who saw no jobs for anyone, and a queue for public housing. – *The Guardian*, 19 March 1992.

It is a pity that 'paleface' appears to be non-PC, as 'person of paleface' would help resolve the problem of what to call a [WHITE MAN].

[paralytic]: See [MENTALLY HANDICAPPED].

parentally disadvantaged: This is the preferred term for an [orphan].

When the time comes for Pan to depart, which of the orphans does he pass his magic sword to? Obviously: the fat black kid (or perhaps I should say the parentally disadvantaged, differently sized Afro-American). – *The Times*, 14 April 1992.

partner: See LOVER and [FIRST LADY].

[passenger]: See RAILSPEAK.

paternally and socially challenged: See -CHALLENGED.

[patients]: In Britain's National Health Service, there are now, properly, no patients, only **clients.** This might appear to be because of the new cost-conscious environment (rather as with 'passengers' in RAILSPEAK), but is rather intended to convey that the client is an active participant who goes to a doctor or specialist with a problem and is not simply a passive [SUFFERER] or [VICTIM].

Hence, there are now 'in-clients' and 'out-clients', at least as far as many social workers, counsellors and psychiatric workers are concerned.

PENILE IMPERIALISM: This concept hardly needs explaining. If no one has invented it yet, they should surely do so. An alternative term for HETEROSEXUAL IMPERIALISM. According to Reisner & Wechsler, *Encyclopedia of Graffiti* (1974), 'Sown with phallic imperialism' was a slogan seen at Berkeley, California, in 1970.

[penis]: See WILLY.

people in poverty: See [POOR].

people of colo(u)r/person of colo(u)r: Meaning 'non-white' – these are terms which have caught on to a considerable degree in the United States but are only just beginning to make a mark in Britain. They are, of course, purposely less specific than 'African-American' or 'Asian-American', though for this reason some people have objected to them on the grounds that they lump all colours together and 'obscure diversity'. The terms are older than they may seem. There are British examples of 'a free person of colour' (1825) and 'married a lady of colour (1907).

The great ambition of students today is to be truly ethical . . . They patiently say 'people of color'. – *The Washington Post*, 17 January 1991.

Reporter Kristi King was castigated for using the phrase 'colored women' instead of the politically correct 'women of color'. – *The Washington Post*, 27 September 1991.

Black, Hispanic and Indian activists, meeting in Washington from October 24th to 27th for the first 'National People of Colour Environmental Leadership Summit', will press this argument in exploring the relationship between environmentalism and racial justice. – *The Economist*, 26 October 1991.

For a while at the beginning of the [Oprah] Winfrey show, everyone . . . talked about 'people of colour', before the hostess herself opted for a blunt 'black'. *The Guardian*, 19 March 1992.

So far, the expression has been largely restricted to America and only used within quotation marks in the UK. Note however:

A public gallery that aims to place 'artists of colour' in a wider contemporary art context is to be set up by the Arts Council and the London Arts Board . . . The Institute of New International Visual Arts . . . sets out to place artists from Africa, the Caribbean and Asia alongside their European and American peers. – *The Independent*, 25 August 1992.

Compare AFRICAN-AMERICAN and [NIGGER].

people/person with differing abilities: This alternative term for DISABLED emerged from 66,000 entries as the winner of a

competition organized by an American charitable group in
1991. Objections to the phrase were soon raised. Dianne Pias-
tro, a syndicated columnist, said the new construction suggested that disablity was somehow shameful and needed to
be treated in a vague generality. Mary Johnson, editor of the
Disability Rag, a disability rights magazine, said, '[It's a] nice
sentiment but it doesn't have any soul. It has no power to it.'
And quite right, too.

people/person with seeing difficulties: See [BLIND].

people with disabilities: See DISABLED.

-person: The intention of putting this suffix in place of '-man' is to
produce sexual neutralization or, at least, to render a word non-
sexist. It is rare, however, for the resultant coinages to be used
unselfconsciously or even with a completely straight face.

> The spokesperson (non-sexist term) for UCWR complained that
> she had been 'physically assaulted by a university administra-
> tor'. – *The Guardian*, 18 February 1972.

> Mrs Sally Oppenheim MP ... [the Conservative] spokesperson on
> consumer affairs. – BBC Radio news, 15 January 1978.

By 1986, *Longman Guardian New Words* was remarking on the
already 'limitless' examples, such as 'barperson', 'bookperson',
'craftsperson', 'houseperson', 'superperson'. A little later, 'state-
sperson' was occasionally used in an almost straightforward
manner.

Then there are the completely humorous inventions, designed
to poke fun at the feminist fad, and which, of course, are definitely
not PC. How about **cowperson** (as in 'cowpersons and native
Americans')? Of these inventions, **personkind** has almost taken
on a life of its own – 'Sonja fights for her life and the lives of all

personkind' (*Video Today*, April 1986) whereas Wagner's **Flying Dutchperson** has not.

(*Sources include: The Daily Telegraph*, 2 October 1991; Vernon Noble, *Speak Softly*, 1982; *The Oxford Dictionary of New Words*, 1991.)

personal attendant: See [CHAMBERMAID].

person living with AIDS: See [-VICTIM].

person of colour: See PEOPLE OF COLO(U)R.

person of ethnicity: A person of a culture other than a EURO-CENTRIC one, and certainly not a D.W.E.M.

person of gender: If it means anything at all, this should denote a human being undistinguished by sex – but it is also used, oddly enough, to denote a woman.

person of non-colour: See [HONKY].

person of restricted growth: For many years, this has been the correct term for a **[dwarf]** or **[midget]**, though it is not included in the *Oxford English Dictionary* (Second Edition), for some reason, nor is there any cautionary label on the word 'dwarf'. The expression first came to general attention when Lord Snowdon made a film on the subject, with the title 'Born to Be Small', for ATV in 1971.

An international dwarf-throwing competition in West Germany next month has been cancelled . . . The Hamburg-based Organisation of People of Restricted Growth protested about what it called a macabre spectacle. – *The Daily Telegraph*, 18 February 1986.

Let us get this absolutely clear: Mickey Rooney is not a dwarf, nor a midget, nor a person of stunted nor restricted nor diminished growth, nor is he waist-high to the average grasshopper. Such opening conversational gambits as 'Hi there, shortie', or

'What's the weather like down in the carpet?' would not be recommended unless you fancy a sharp head-butt in the ankle. – *The Times*, 15 March 1992.

In consequence, consider renaming the fairytale, 'Snow White and the Seven Persons of Restricted Growth'.

(*Sources include: Longman Guardian New Words*, 1986.)

person of size: See [FAT].

person of substance: See [FAT].

personhole: See FEMHOLE.

person with –: See DISABLED and [-VICTIM].

person with a drink problem: See [ALCOHOLIC].

[pet]: See ANIMAL COMPANION and HOUSEHOLD NON-HUMAN ANIMAL.

PHALLOCENTRICISM/PHALLOCENTRICITY: The male view of life, the universe and everything. Similar to HETEROSEXUAL or PENILE IMPERIALISM, and particularly prevalent in literature.

Columnists hoot at news of students . . . decrying Shakespeare's 'phallocentric' vision. – *The Washington Post*, 3 February 1991.

There is also a coinage **phallogocentric**, implying a male tyranny through language, which Terry Eagleton in *Introduction to Literary Theory* glosses as 'cocksure'.

physically challenged: See -CHALLENGED and DISABLED.

physically different: See DISABLED.

[physically handicapped]: See DISABLED.

physiologically disenfranchised: See DISABLED.

[piano accompanist]: See [ACCOMPANIST, PIANO].

pilot: See [AIRMAN/AIRWOMAN].

plain indians/Plains Indian: See [RED INDIAN].

[plump]: See [FAT].

poet: And see [-ESS SUFFIX].

[Polack]: Since at least the 1890s, this has been a term of disparagement used in North America for a Polish immigrant or any person of Polish descent. **Polish** is not a longer word and is the only substitute.

[police cell]: See CUSTODY SUITE.

[policeman]: To be avoided by the non-sexist. After all, 'Policewomen are often involved. Police, police officers, detectives, policemen and women can be used.' – 'Guidelines for Factual Programmes', BBC (1989).

poof/poofter/poove etc.: See GAY.

[poor, the]: Instead of this unfortunate phrase, consider using **deprived/disadvantaged people, those in the lower income bracket** (originally an advertising classification but adopted by politicians), or the **underprivileged.** Also **people in poverty. Economically exploited** has apparently replaced **[economically disadvantaged]**, which blames the victim rather than the oppressor. Then there is the quintessentially PC **differently advantaged.**

(*Sources include:* Vernon Noble, *Speak Softly – Euphemisms and Such*, 1982; *The Sunday Telegraph*, 27 October 1991; Beard & Cerf, *The Official Politically Correct Dictionary and Handbook*, 1992.)

positive discrimination: The favouring of groups considered to be underprivileged – or unfair discrimination in support of an oppressed minority (depending on where you are standing). An expression familiar by 1967 in the UK.

With this victory over the successors of the once mighty Lords Commissioners of the Admiralty, in forcing them into this blatant sex discrimination (or, in politically correct language, positive discrimination), I cannot understand why the feminists are getting so excited about a small skirmish like membership of the Garrick Club. All they should do – as would any commander on encountering a pocket of resistance – is leave it behind in their drive towards superiority, and return to starve it out or beat it into submission at a later date. – *The Daily Telegraph*, 15 July 1992.

See also EQUAL OPPORTUNITY.

positive images: What the PC would always like to see – as opposed, naturally, to **negative images.**

Basic Instinct is condemned for its portrayal of gays – as if positive images would make everything all right ... A generation of political activists have devoted all their energy to improving the condition of blacks, women and gays in the fictional worlds thrown up by mass culture – while neglecting the causes of discrimination in the real world. – *The Guardian*, 7 May 1992.

[powerless]: See DISEMPOWERED.

presenter: See [ANCHORMAN].

Presidential Partner: See [FIRST LADY].

pre-woman/pre-women: See [GIRL(S)].

print-handicapped: A term used for people who are unable to read books or any other printed matter. They may learn more easily from audio and video sources.

Children who are 'print-handicapped' [might] . . . have a sight problem or . . . a physical disability that precludes them from turning pages. – *The Guardian*, 19 July 1988.

[prisoner]: Preferable PC phrases from America include **client of the correctional system** and **guest in a correctional institution.** Compare the time-honoured British expression that someone in prison is 'detained at Her Majesty's pleasure'.
See also CUSTODY SUITE.

(*Sources include:* Beard & Cerf, *The Official Politically Correct Dictionary and Handbook*, 1992.)

problem drinker: See [ALCOHOLIC].

profoundly deaf: See [DEAF].

[**prostitute**]: See SEX WORKER.

public official: See [ALDERMAN].

[**putting on weight**]: See [FAT].

P.W.A.: (Person With AIDS). See [-VICTIM].

Q

queer: See GAY.

R

RACISM/RACIALISM: Although the idea is, presumably, as old as humankind, the word 'racialism' is not recorded until 1907; 'racism' not until 1936.

See also UNCLE TOM(M)ISM.

RACIST/RACIALIST: Whichever form you use, the mother of all '-ists' had come into use by 1932.

RAILSPEAK: The rewriting of the dictionary by British Rail, in order to make its passengers view the railway system in the way BR desires it to be seen, qualifies for this book because of the coercion involved. If one wanted to name this sort of terminology it would better be termed BC – for 'bureaucratic correctness'.

The most significant changes are these: **[passengers]** are now **customers**; **[guards]** are **senior conductors**; **[tickets]** are **travel documents**; **[coaches]** have become **accommodation** (as in 'towards the rear of the First Class accommodation'); and plain old-fashioned **[stops]** became by 1986, curiously, **station stops**. For all one knows, there may be plans to call drivers 'pilots', as clearly the whole drift is to make travelling by train seem as superficially glamorous as air travel.

In October 1992, I received the disturbing news that British Rail had started to call some of its stations **travel centres**.

[railwaymen]: 'Same difficulties over National Union of Railwaymen as with National Union of Seamen [see SEAMEN]. Scripts can refer to the main railway union, the NUR.' – 'Guidelines for Factual Programmes', BBC (1989).

[rain, threat of]: During a drought, American TV weather-forecasters had to adopt PC terminology. They had to talk about the **hope of rain** or the **promise of rain.**

(*Source: The Daily Telegraph,* 14 January 1991.)

rainbow culture: What results from the banding together of **rainbow minorities,** i.e. particularly those distinguished by being of an array of colours. These expressions developed from the 'Rainbow Coalition' of minority peoples – 'the Blacks, the browns, the white liberals, and the Yellow Dog Democrats' who united in US politics around 1982.

Such populism has been fuelled by a feeling that Washington and the liberal establishment, the national media and the Democrats in Congress are ignoring the concerns of [whites] for fear of antagonising 'rainbow' minorities. – *The Times,* 16 November 1991.

The new multiculturism is not just demanding a place in a rainbow culture, it is insisting on a redefinition of the rainbow in which the old white Anglo-Saxon colonial segment would be given subservient status, and perhaps might even be rubbed out altogether. – *The Guardian,* 5 March 1992.

rape, acquaintance/date: See DATE RAPE.

[rat-catcher]: See RODENT OFFICER/OPERATOR.

recovering racists: A term given to people who have seen the PC light, realize they are racists and are trying to reform.

[Red Indian]: As a name for the original inhabitants of North America, this term has never been acceptable (not least because the colour description seems curiously inaccurate). Since the 1730s at least, the *correct* term has been **Native American** though this has often been used in a very general sense about old inhabitants of the North American continent. Since the 1970s, however, it has become the specifically correct term for 'Red Indians'.

Appearing at the [Academy] awards in Brando's behalf was the beautiful, gracious, and now famous Native American woman, Sacheen Littlefeather, who, dressed in the traditional garments of her people, read a prepared statement. – *Black Panther*, 7 April 1973.

Political correctness seems to have infiltrated the BBC. This week's issue of *BBC Playdays*, the corporation's magazine for kids, contains detailed instructions on how to make a headdress using only thin card, glue and feathers. 'Now you can pretend to be native Americans,' it enthuses. – *The Times*, 5 February 1992.

Never mind the pejorative sense often found in the term [NATIVES], **Native American** is still very much the PC term. Equally acceptable, though requiring more precise usage, are the terms **plain indians** or **Plains Indian.** These refer to the former Indian inhabitants of the North American plains (and have been so used since the seventeenth century).

Alternative forms are **(North) American Indian** or **Amerindian**, though, for whatever reason, these are less popular.

Up with the Asians and Amerindians, down with the Europeans. Up the natives, down with the colonists if they are white, that is. – *The Times*, 2 November 1991.

Bruce Beresford's *Black Robe* . . . has won critical plaudits but was attacked by American Indian leaders for showing 'savage hostility – not (their) culture.' – *The Independent*, 24 January 1992.

Will the dictates of political correctness force the Washington Redskins, victors of the Super Bowl, to change their name? After their triumph over the Buffalo Bills on Sunday night, the American Indian Movement was demanding that the team make the change. – *The Times*, 28 January 1992.

There is a rights organization called the American Indian Movement. It should be noted, however, that all groups including the term 'American' fall foul of the fact that the word was introduced from Europe (after the Italian Amerigo Vespucci), which simply won't do if EUROCENTRISM and D.W.E.M.S are to be avoided. It is much safer to refer to the members of a specific Indian 'nation' – Cherokee, Navajo, or whatever.

A joke nonce-coinage in 'The Way of the World' column in *The Daily Telegraph* (2 December 1991) was 'quasi-autochthonous American Indigenes'.

refuse collector/refuse disposal operative: Long before PC was invented, great minds were bent on elevating the name given to the inevitably menial job of the **[dust(bin)man]**. Other attempts to find new terms ground to a halt with **sanitary assistant**.

> It happened to the rat-catcher (he's now a rodent operator), the dustman (refuse collector), and the sweeper (street orderly). – *The Daily Mail*, 25 October 1958.

[retarded]: See [MENTALLY HANDICAPPED].

[retirement]: (from work). Euphemisms for this stage in life have included 'the leisure years' and 'the longest holiday', but there does not seem to be a term with the PC seal of approval.

See also [SACK, THE].

right on: According to Stuart Berg Flexner in *I Hear America Talking* (1976), 'Right on!' replaced 'Tell it like it is!' as the Civil Rights shout of encouragement to speakers at demonstrations round about 1967. It is 'a general term meaning "you're absolutely right, you tell 'em".' The *Oxford English Dictionary* (Second Edition) finds, however, a 1925 Negro use of the phrase.

More recently, the phrase has come to refer to certain attitudes that might equally qualify for the designation 'politically correct'.

> My play takes a sledgehammer to the 'right on' clichés that have debilitated recent radical theatre in Britain. – *The Guardian*, 7 April 1992.

[riper years, of]: See THIRD AGE.

ritual abuse: See -ABUSE.

[-RIX SUFFIX]: As with the [-ESS SUFFIX], resistance to this Latin female form results as much from the awkward nature of the words as from any sexism involved in their use. Who in their right minds would wish to refer to Amy Johnson as an **[aviatrix]** rather than an **aviator, pilot,** or **flier,** or to any female **editor** as an **[editrix]** – except in jest?

[roadsweeper]: See STREET ORDERLY.

rodent officer/operator/operative: An early form of PC was presumably at work when a **[rat-catcher]** was so renamed. See the Introduction.

Westminster City Council's rat-catcher is in future to be called Rodent Officer. – *The Liverpool Echo*, 31 January 1944.

When it comes to official jargon, can you beat turning our old friend the rat-catcher into a 'Rodent Operative'? – *The Sunday Times*, 5 November 1944.

Euphemisms . . . *rodent operator* for *rat-catcher.* – *Word Study*, May 1946.

It happened to the rat-catcher (he's now a rodent operator), the dustman (refuse collector), and the sweeper (street orderly). – *The Daily Mail*, 25 October 1958.

(*Source: The Oxford English Dictionary*, Second Edition.)

S

[sack, the]: People are 'asked to step down' and accept 'voluntary redundancy', or their 'services are dispensed with' and they are told 'I'm afraid we shall have to let you go'. Bureaucratic euphemism also runs to 'reduction of staff(ing) levels' and 'termination of employment'. 'Rationalize' was a word coined in the 1970s for weeding-out, but what is the PC term for this sort of thing?

(*Sources include:* Vernon Noble, *Speak Softly – Euphemisms and Such*, 1982.)

[sado-masochistic]: Consider **the differently pleasured** – a joke coinage from *The New York Times*, July 1992, but almost certainly more seriously intended when earlier employed by Julia Penelope in *Speaking Freely* (New York, 1990).

sanitary assistant: See REFUSE COLLECTOR.

satanic abuse: See -ABUSE.

SCENTISM: Inflicting one's perfume or aftershave on others who may be allergic to it – though not, apparently, discrimination and prejudice against people who do this (for which, see SMELLISM).

(*Source:* Beard & Cerf, *The Official Politically Correct Dictionary and Handbook*, 1992.)

[seamen]: 'Slightly tricky since the National Union of Seamen insist on the title though they have women members. Even so sailors and union members are appropriate.' – 'Guidelines for Factual Programmes', BBC (1989).

seasoned: See [OLD].

self-inflicted death: See [SUICIDE].

[seminar]: The *New York Review of Books* reported that a US professor refused to lead seminars and held 'ovulars' instead. (Quoted by Flora Lewis, *The International Herald Tribune*, 12 July 1991.)

senior citizen: See [OLD].

senior conductor: See RAILSPEAK.

servant: See [CHAMBERMAID].

[sex change]: The OK term used by a London hospital in the early 1980s was **gender reassignment** and this is now the PC term.

> Myka Scott (né Michael Scott) is a pre-op transsexual . . . [and] doesn't like the term 'sex change', preferring 'gender reassignment operation'. – *The Independent*, 22 August 1992.

(*Sources include:* Vernon Noble, *Speak Softly – Euphemisms and Such*, 1982.)

SEXISM: Prejudice or discrimination against a person (usually female) on the grounds of sex. The most significant -ISM in the field of political correctness, with the possible exception of RACISM.

SEXUAL NEUTRALIZATION: See -PERSON.

sex worker: Use instead of **[prostitute]**. Another example – probably – of bureaucratic euphemism that has become PC. It may also be a way of heading off sexism into the bargain, as a 'prostitute' is invariably taken as female ('male prostitute' being employed, pointedly, for those of the other sex).

> Now we are promised a campaign against prostitutes, or 'sex workers', as our officialdom puts it. – *The Sunday Telegraph*, 23 July 1989.

(*Sources include: The Longman Register of New Words*, 1990; Jane Mills, *Womanwords*, 1991).

shopper: See [HOUSEWIFE].

[shopping-bag lady]: See [BAG LADY/BAGLADY].

[short]: See -CHALLENGED and VERTICALLY IMPAIRED. .

SIGHTISM: Prejudice or discrimination against the blind, according to *The Times*, 30 June 1992, though it is not clear what form it takes. Presumably, in a reluctance to give employment and other opportunities to the blind. Possibly the term could be extended to include prejudice against those who wear spectacles.

[silly ass]: See ANIMALISM.

significant other: As though LOVER or 'partner' were thought to be too revealing (while yet remaining wonderfully imprecise as to legal status), someone came along and suggested this even vaguer term. Often given capitals, Significant Other was in existence by 9 November 1986, when it was discussed by William Safire in *The New York Times Magazine*.

single-by-choice: See [SPINSTER].

[single parent]: Describing a person who is bringing up a child without the assistance of a marital partner, this term has been current since 1969. Now, however, Gingerbread, the UK organization catering for people in that position, prefers the term **lone parent**. This is because 'single' may suggest 'unmarried' when it is hardly relevant whether the parents are married or not. The point is that the lone parent is on his or her own because of divorce, desertion, separation or death, or because the partner is in hospital or prison.

single woman: See [BACHELOR GIRL/BACHELORETTE].

SIZIST/SIZEIST: Prejudice or discrimination against people because of their size – that is, weight and/or height – insofar as it differs from a perceived norm.

Minorco's chief executive, Sir Michael Edwardes (5ft 4in) started the battle for Consolidated Gold Fields with 30% of its equity. He still failed to take it. ConsGold's boss Mr Randolph Agnew (6ft 1in) often mimicked Sir Michael's gait in what can only be described as a sizist way. – *The Economist*, 19 August 1989.

Compare HEIGHTIST, WEIGHTIST.

(*Sources include: The Longman Register of New Words*, 1990.)

[slave]: Should be **enslaved person**, according to a report entitled 'One Nation; Many Peoples: a Declaration of Cultural Independence' issued by the New York State Board of Education (June 1991). Presumably this is because a slave is just a slave, but an 'enslaved person' has been brought to this condition by an oppressor. In addition, the new term draws attention to the *person* as much as to the condition.

(*Source: The Independent*, 8 July 1991.)

slow learner: See [MENTALLY HANDICAPPED].

[small]: Use **differently heighted**, as suggested in *The Times*, 28 June 1992.

Consider also VERTICALLY IMPAIRED and 'vertically challenged' (see -CHALLENGED).

SMELLISM: Prejudice or discrimination against people on the strength of their body odour.

Compare SCENTISM.

[smelly]: See HYGIENICALLY CHALLENGED.

SMOKEISM: Persecution or discrimination against smokers by non-smokers – a phrase coined by Keith Waterhouse in his *Daily Mirror* column before 1986.

See also -ISM.

[snowman]: The non-sexist form is not, apparently 'snowperson', as you might expect, but 'snow figure/sculpture/creature, snow-woman *or* snowman *if it really is*'. (Rosalie Maggio, *The Nonsexist Word Finder: A Dictionary of Gender-Free Usage*, Boston, Mass., 1988.) As for **[abominable snowman]**, use instead the alternative Tibetan term *Yeti*.

solvent abuse: See -ABUSE.

[spade]: Generally considered an offensive term for a black person – and presumably derived from the expression 'as black as the ace of spades'. Current by 1919, according to Stuart Berg Flexner, *I Hear America Talking* (1976), and 'seems to have been prison slang for a very dark-complected Black.'
   See also [DORIS].

Spanish-speaking: See HISPANIC.

[spastic]: See CEREBRAL PALSY.

special: See [MENTALLY HANDICAPPED].

special man: See GAY.

special needs, with: See [MENTALLY HANDICAPPED].

SPECISM/SPECIESISM: The original form was 'speciesism', coined some time in the mid-1970s to describe human discrimination against animals. The shorter 'specism' had arrived by 1985. The concept is similar to ANIMALISM, in that opponents of speciesism believe that animals, too, have rights. Not quite the same as the old 'cruelty to animals', though that may come into it. The International Fund for Animal Welfare campaigns in particular against the eating of cats and dogs, which is a SPECIST thing to do, though just as bad as doing it to any other kind of animal.

SPECIST: A person who behaves according to the dictates of SPECISM/SPECIESISM.

[spic]: See HISPANIC.

[spiggoty]: See HISPANIC.

[spinster]: Avoid this appellation at all costs and use, rather, **single-by-choice.** Hence any **[old maid]** is, rather, a 'single-by-choice senior citizen'.

(*Source*: *The Sunday Telegraph*, 8 March 1992.)

[spokesman]: The term **spokesperson** has had some life (see -PERSON), but the 'Guidelines for Factual Programmes', BBC (1989), recommend **company representative** – 'or refer to a "company statement" instead if appropriate.'

staffing: To be used in preference to **[manning]**, according to the 'Guidelines for Factual Programmes', BBC (1989). Also 'jobs', 'job levels' will do the non-sexist trick.

station stop: See RAILSPEAK.

sterile: See [BARREN].

steward/[stewardess]: See [-ESS SUFFIX] and FLIGHT ATTENDANT.

[stop]: See RAILSPEAK.

[stout]: See [FAT].

STOUTISM: See FATISM.

street orderly: However unlikely a name, this is what you should call a **[roadsweeper]**. The street orderly has a long and distinguished history. 'Street orderly bins' were known by the 1890s and were so called after an 'orderly plan' for keeping the streets continually swept had been instituted. **Street sweeper**, though known in the US, is barely used in the UK.

See also REFUSE COLLECTOR.

street person: See [BAG LADY].

[stricken by]: See DISABLED.

[sub-fertility problem]: See [BARREN].

[subnormal]: See [MENTALLY HANDICAPPED].

substance abuse: See -ABUSE.

[sufferer/suffering from]: [PATIENTS] of whatever type must never be said to 'suffer' from any disease or condition, any more than they can become a [VICTIM] of it.

> Saying that a person 'suffers' from multiple sclerosis is often not based on an awareness of either the impact of the disease on that person's life, or of their attitude towards it. Many people simply regard the difficulties associated with their disabilities as a normal part of life. This should not be portrayed as 'heroic stoicism' but as an assertion of the normality of disability. – Briefing Note, The Royal Association for Disability and Rehabilitation, May 1992.

See also DISABLED and [MAD].

[suffragette]/suffragist: See [-ETTE SUFFIX].

[suicide]: Marginally more positive are such euphemisms as **auto-euthanasia** (simply the lesser-known Greek form of the word), **self-inflicted death** and **voluntary death.**

> I would like to represent this voluntary death as an exemplary case. – Peter Handke (on the death by suicide of his mother), *A Sorrow Beyond Dreams* (1976).

> Shaw was then 83, Mrs [Virginia] Woolf in her late 50s and within a year of her self-inflicted death. – *Radio Times*, May 1977.

'Suicide' has long disappeared as an inquest verdict – hence such formulations as, 'He took his life while the balance of his mind was disturbed'.

(*Source:* Vernon Noble, *Speak Softly – Euphemisms and Such*, 1982.)

[sunset days]: See THIRD AGE.

survivor: See [-VICTIM].

[swapping sex partners]: See CONSENSUAL NON-MONOGAMY.

T

[tall]: See -CHALLENGED and VERTICALLY IMPAIRED.

tax inspector: To be used instead of the sexist **[taxman]**, because it is also accurate, according to the 'Guidelines for Factual Programmes', BBC (1989). Not that such an easy adjustment can be effected with [POLICEMAN], except where appropriate, of course. 'Use also the Inland Revenue and Revenue staff', the Guide goes on.

TEMPORALLY/TEMPORARILY ABLE(D): What hitherto we may have thought of as 'able(d)'. A menacing, Orwellian coinage designed to make those who are not disabled realize that they could become so at any moment. It seems to be saying that it is only a question of time – though there seems to be a certain amount of doubt as to which adverb is intended. In the form 'temporarily able', it was noted by Jerry Ardler *et al.*, 'Thought Police', *Newsweek*, 14 January 1991.

(*Other source: The Daily Telegraph*, 29 May 1991.)

terminological inexactitude: See COUNTER-FACTUAL PROPOSITION.

Third Age, the: This is the most successful of the euphemisms for 'old age', but is not widely used. Of French origin (*troisième âge*), the phrase can also be used specifically to refer to retirement. The University of the Third Age – set up for retired people in France by Pierre Vellus in 1973 – has also been introduced to the UK. Learning is for pleasure: there are no qualifications, examinations or age limits.

The phrase 'the third age of your life' had been used earlier – much earlier – in 1446, in English.

Objection would no doubt be raised against most of the other poetic euphemisms: the Prayer Book's **[of riper years]**, not to mention **[later years]**, **[sunset years]**, **[twilight years]**, and **[vintage years]** (this last, an Americanism). The Japanese have a more elegant turn of phrase. 'Old age used to be known as the "silver age". Now jitsunen, meaning the "age of fruition" is replacing it.' (*The Times*, 22 January 1992.)

See also [OLD].

(*Sources include:* Vernon Noble, *Speak Softly – Euphemisms and Such*, 1982.)

Third World, the: An early example of PC-speak, coined in French in 1956, to describe the DEVELOPING COUNTRIES generally not aligned with the Communist and non-Communist blocs. Hence also, to describe the same phenomenon, the term 'non-aligned nations'.

[ticket]: See RAILSPEAK.

TOKENISM: Originally used in the US to describe a certain half-hearted, window-dressing approach to racial integration(by 1962), this has come to be used to describe any form of 'gesture politics', for example, the placing of one woman or gay or black on a committee, just to show willing. This can be patronizing, to say the least. It is practised by companies, schools, sports teams etc. who appear to abide by equal-opportunity laws by accepting a token representation of minority groups, especially blacks or women. A 'showcase nigger' is black slang for a token black given high visibility in the company's front office.

As you know quizzes are often criticized by feminists for having what's called a 'token woman' on the panel. Well, we entirely sympathize with that view. So this week we've got no women on the panel at all. – *Quote . . . Unquote*, BBC Radio, May 1978.

We are told that we must have more women in science and that we can get them there by creating female-friendly science classes. I wonder why? Is it a question of quotas? Is it sheer bloody-minded tokenism? – *The Sunday Telegraph*, 23 February 1992.

[tramp]: In the sense of **[vagrant]** or beggar, patronizing euphemisms such as **[gentleman of the road]** will not do.

Gentlemen of the road get first-class accommodation plus medical care costing up to £100 a week or more [under the National Health Service]. – *The Guardian*, 21 April 1975.

Nor is it acceptable to use **[down-and-out]**, which was originally an American expression and known by the end of the nineteenth century.

'His need is greater than mine. I just hope he doesn't mind the mustard my wife put in them.' Magistrate Dudley Thomas, who gave his lunch to a down-and-out appearing before him. *The Independent*, 22 August 1992.

'Vagrant', an old word with its connotations of 'wandering', seems harmless enough, but nowadays sounds pejorative, so must be ruled non-PC. There is no very acceptable phrase.
Compare [BAG LADY/BAGLADY].

(*Sources include:* Vernon Noble, *Speak Softly – Euphemisms and Such*, 1982.)

travel centre: See RAILSPEAK.

travel document: See RAILSPEAK.

travellers: See [GYPSY].

trichologically challenged: See -CHALLENGED.

tropical rain forests: See [JUNGLE].

[twilight years]: See THIRD AGE.

U

[ugly]: For this, use cosmetically different and see -CHALLENGED.

UGLYISM: Discrimination or prejudice against a person (usually, though it could be directed at animals) on the grounds of unfavourable appearance.

> The ultimate sanction of the politically correct will be enacted in a California town this week when it prohibits discrimination against people who are ugly. Uglyism has come to the town of Santa Cruz, a seaside enclave 75 miles south of San Francisco that offers nude beaches and is home to ageing hippies, trendy computer hackers, health food nuts ... – *The Guardian*, 26 May 1992.

UNCLE TOM(M)ISM: Discussing Harriet Beecher Stowe's novel *Uncle Tom's Cabin* (1852), *The Oxford Companion to English Literature* (1985) notes how the book's original sensational success was replaced by a 'shift of attitude which came to use the phrase "Uncle Tom" pejoratively, to indicate a supine collaboration with the oppressor.' As such, it is plain that what we have here is an early form of politically incorrect behaviour. Uncle Tom is too pious for his own good – indeed, eventually and unprotestingly, he gets beaten to death by the slave-owner, Simon Legree.

Taking various forms – 'Uncle Tom(m)ery' 'Uncle Tom(m)ing' and 'Uncle Tom(m)ishness' – the concept was being commented on by the 1930s:

> Uncle Tomism, acceptance, toadying – all there in its most rugged form. One way to be a nigger. Other negroes did it other

ways – he did it the hard way. The same result – *a nigger*. – Chester Himes, *Black on Black* (1937).

underachievement/underachiever: More positive ways of describing lack of success and failures in the race of life. Both words were known by the early 1950s, chiefly in use by educational psychologists.

[underdeveloped countries]: See DEVELOPING COUNTRIES.

underprivileged: See [POOR].

[unemployed]: Substitute **involuntarily leisured.**

uniquely abled: See -ABLED and DISABLED.

university challenged: See -CHALLENGED.

unmarried woman: See [BACHELOR GIRL/BACHELORETTE].

unseeing person: See [BLIND].

unwaged: Sometimes a marginally more dignified way of saying 'out of work', at others, a means of recognizing the contribution to society made by people (like non-working mothers) who do not receive wages.

The cost will be £2 per line for waged persons or £1 per line for those who are unwaged. – *Library Association Record*, 30 November 1982.

(*Source: The Oxford Dictionary of New Words*, 1991.)

V

vagina: This is totally PC – not least because there is no other right-on term.

> The real reason... why women are loath to describe their private parts must surely be that there is no acceptable word. There is no female equivalent of the unthreatening, used-by-all 'Willy', although new words have been suggested. Feminist linguist Deborah Cameron suggests 'ginny' pronounced with a 'j' sound, a nicely inoffensive abreviation of vagina. – *The Guardian*, 9 July 1992.

See also WILLY.

[vagrant]: See [TRAMP].

[vegetable]: See [MENTALLY HANDICAPPED].

verbal hygiene: An approach to language that is both positive and negative.

> 'Verbal hygiene' is ultimately the after-echo of the primal big bang of language, that disruptive event at the Tower of Babel. It is a blessing as well as a curse. It is an impulse which can work to eradicate the traces of old intolerances from language, or to implant the stigmata of new intolerances, as in the extremes of the modern 'political correctness' movement.– *The Times*, 20 May 1992.

verbally challenged: See -CHALLENGED.

vertically challenged: See -CHALLENGED.

vertically impaired: A joke expression for 'short', [SMALL] or even 'tall'.

victim: The object of an OPPRESSOR. However:

[-victim]/[victim of]: As with **[-sufferer]** and **[patient]**, particularly when used in conjunction with 'AIDS', this is non-PC usage. The acceptable alternatives include, for example, **person with AIDS** and **person living with AIDS**, often abbreviated to **PWA, PLA** or **PLWA**. The emphasis in these alternatives is designed to show that the people are 'living with' rather than 'dying from' AIDS. At the second AIDS forum in the US, held at Denver, Colorado, in December 1983, a statement was issued, saying: 'We condemn attempts to label us as "victims", which implies defeat, and we are only occasionally "patients", which implies passivity, helplessness, and dependence upon the care of others.'

For the same reasons, the word 'victim' should not be used of any other person with mental or physical illness or handicap. Hence, 'Jane Smith **has/has contracted polio**.' As the Briefing Note (May 1992) from the Royal Association for Disability and Rehabilitation, puts it: 'Instead use the phrases "someone who has" or "a person with" a disease or disability. These phrases are more neutral and less value-laden.'

[-Infected] is also negative:

Lesbian Feminist Liz Abzug Running Against HIV-Infected Activist For City Council Seat. – Headline, *The Washington Post*, 11 September 1991.

Note also the positive PC qualities of the word **survivor:**

On the frontiers of political correctness and social sensitivity, a rape victim is not a rape victim, but a 'rape survivor'. – *The Washington Post*, 22 November 1991.

See also DISABLED.

(*Sources include: The Oxford Dictionary of New Words*, 1991.)

[vintage years]: See THIRD AGE.

visually challenged: See -CHALLENGED.

visually impaired individual: See [BLIND].

W

waiter/[waitress]: See WAITPERSON.

waitperson: An American non-sexist coinage for **waiter** or
[waitress]. There is nothing wrong with using 'waiter' to apply
to a male or female, but 'waitperson' does have a certain amount
of use.

> It is the only caffeinated coffee served by the 'wait-persons', as
> they are called, at the politically correct Takoma Cafe in Takoma
> Park. – *The Washington Post*, 11 March 1985.

> Waitperson wanted ... Olive Tree Cafe. – *Village Voice*, 14 June
> 1988.

Another attempt was **waitron** but this one never seemed to get off
the launching pad.

(*Sources include: The Longman Register of New Words*, 1990.)

WEIGHTISM: Discrimination or prejudice against a person on the
grounds of (usually) excessive weight.

> Big is not beautiful, formerly fat models tell of weightism. – *The
> Independent*, 25 May 1989.

Compare FATISM.

(*Source: The Longman Register of New Words*, 1990.)

[well-built]: See [FAT].

[well-endowed]: See [FAT].

wheelchair user: The PC term. **Person in a wheelchair** is also acceptable, but phrases to the effect that someone is **[confined to a wheelchair]** or **[wheelchair-bound]** should not be used. The point is that 'wheelchairs liberate rather confine' and it is unlikely that anybody spends all day in one, anyway. **Wheelchair accessible** is positive in this connection, and therefore acceptable.

I am fortunate enough not to be wheelchair-bound. – *The Daily Mail*, 17 June 1981.

As a person in a wheelchair, I read with interest the article on physicist Stephen Hawking and his severe disability. I was disappointed, however, to see you refer to him as 'confined to a wheelchair, a virtual prisoner in his own body'. The expression 'confined to a wheelchair', though common, is misleading and insulting. Wheelchairs are tools that enable us to get around. They are liberating, not confining. As for his being a 'prisoner in his own body', who is not? – Letter to *Time*, 29 February 1988.

If you are reporting the difficulties confronting a disabled individual or group, do not merely focus on the individual's physical or mental impairments, but upon the broader social causes of the problems, e.g. the inaccessible social environment for wheelchair users ... Do not write 'confined to a wheelchair'. Instead describe a person as a 'wheelchair user'. From their point of view (which is the important one) a wheelchair is an aid to mobility, not a restriction. – Briefing Note, The Royal Association for Disability and Rehabilitation, May 1992.

[white Australian]: See ABORIGINAL/ABORIGINE.

[white coffee]: For obvious reasons, orders should be given for **coffee with milk**; for [black coffee] order **coffee without milk**.

[white man]: Instead, use **white person** or **Caucasian** or, if you want to make a point, **person of non-colour**.

[In the US] It is becoming offensive to use the term 'white' to refer to the species the police define as caucasians . . . Instead of white, you are now advised to say 'non-African-American' or 'non-American-Indian'. At the worst, 'European-American' is acceptable. – *The Times*, 6 November 1990.

widen the circle, to: Very PC term for opening up an area for discussion or broadening the topic.

willy: This much-used (mostly British) term is probably PC because it effectively reduces the **[penis]** (a tool of oppression) to the level of a harmless joke. On the other hand, as PCPs are not renowned for their sense of humour, perhaps a more appropriate word is in the pipeline.
See also VAGINA.

wimmin: This is a point-making feminist neologism to remove the 'men' element from the word 'women' (compare HERSTORY). It is highly irritating to many men and a coinage that has come to be associated with extreme feminism. *Private Eye* started a column poking fun at feminist abuses, entitled 'Wimmin' in 1983.

The word is sometimes spelt **womyn**, which makes a singular use easier. *The Oxford Dictionary of New Words* (1991) cites an unnamed feminist dictionary quoting an unnamed feminist magazine 'for, about, and by young wimmin' as saying, 'We have spelt it this way because we are not wo*men* neither are we fe*male* . . . You may find it trivial – it's just another part of the deep, very deep-rooted sexist attitudes.'

In fact, the source was *A Feminist Dictionary* by Kramarae & Treichler (Boston, 1985) and the magazine was actually called *This Magazine Is For, About, and By Young Wimmin.* Still, a date for the coinage is lacking.

'Wimmin have reclaimed the earth . . .' 'Why wimmin?' 'We want to spell women in a way that does not spell men.' – *The Observer*, 13 March 1983.

[with a mature figure]: See [FAT].

[with surplus weight]: See [FAT].

[wog]: What one might call the traditional British term of abuse for members of the darker, particularly Arab, races (especially of the Empire) is, of course, completely unacceptable nowadays. However, as with **bent** and [NIGGER], it still has a certain currency among those to whom it was formerly applied. In August 1992, Boutros Boutros-Ghali, the Egyptian-born Secretary-General of the United Nations, gave a newspaper interview in which he passed on his explanation for the difficulties he was having at that time with the British Government. 'Maybe [it's] because I'm a wog,' he said, and caused a good deal of tut-tutting round the globe. One of the reasons for his difficulties with the British was that they believed he was too old for his job. His use of outdated slang, harking back to colonial animosities between his country and Britain, only seemed to confirm this.

It has been said that the word derives from clothing stamped with the initials for 'Worn On Government Service', or with some similar acronym, but evidence is lacking. Curiously, the *OED2* does not find a citation earlier than the 1920s.

woman, single/unmarried: See [BACHELOR GIRL/BACHELORETTE].

woman, to: A dubious coinage to avoid using the verb 'to man'. Obviously 'to person' was thought unconvincing. Hardly ever used, but it was, semi-seriously, in this newspaper report:

Later this month the stretch of river alongside the Palace of Westminster will witness a unique event: a charity regatta in which dozens of boats manned (and womanned) by various Parliamentary groups will compete. – *The Guardian*, 4 July 1986.

The verb 'to woman' has also been used, occasionally, in other senses since the sixteenth century, including 'to behave like a woman' and 'to deprive of virginity'.

(*Sources: The Oxford English Dictionary*, Second Edition; *The Longman Register of New Words*, 1989.)

WOMANISM: See WOMANIST.

WOMANIST: An alternative name for a FEMINIST, used mostly by or about black feminists in the US, and used to describe a woman who prefers female company without wishing to exclude men. Coined by the writer Alice Walker.

Women who love other women, yes, but women who also have concern, in a culture that oppresses all black people (and this would go back very far), for their fathers, brothers, and sons, no matter how they feel about them as males. My own terms for such women would be 'womanist' . . . It would have to be a word that affirmed connectedness to the entire community and the world. – Alice Walker, *In Search of Our Mother's Gardens* (1983).

A gifted, prolific writer, [Alice] Walker has called herself a 'womanist'. Her novel The Color Purple won a Pulitzer Prize for fiction in 1983. – *National Geographic*, August 1989.

The word **WOMANISM**, as an alternative to FEMINISM ('advocacy or enthusiasm for the rights, achievements of women', according to *The Oxford English Dictionary*, Second Edition), was current by the 1860s. In the seventeenth century, a 'womanist' was a man who was what we would now call a 'womanizer'.

(*Sources include: The Longman Register of New Words*, 1990.)

womyn: See WIMMIN.

[wop]: A more racist term than [EYETIE] for an Italian, but also applied to other southern Europeans. It was known in the US by 1912.

Y

[yid]: See JEWISH.

Bibliography

Bibliography

Ayto, John, *The Longman Register of New Words*, Longman Group UK, Vol.1 1989, Vol.2 1990.

Beard, Henry & Cerf, Christopher, *The Official Politically Correct Dictionary & Handbook*, Villard Books, New York, 1992.

'Definitions', Smith College Office of Student Affairs, 1990.

Dumond, Val, *The Elements of Nonsexist Usage*, Prentice Hall Press, New York, 1990.

'Guidelines for Factual Programmes', BBC, London, 1989.

'Guide to the Representation of People With Disabilities in Programmes' compiled by Geoffrey Prout, BBC, London, 1990.

'Improving Media Images of Disability', Briefing Note of The Royal Association for Disability and Rehabilitation, May London, 1992.

Jewett, Claudia L., *Adopting the Older Child*, Harvard Common Press, Boston, Mass., 1978.

King, Ruth (ed.), *Talking Gender: A Guide to Nonsexist Communication*, Copp Clark Pitman Ltd, Toronto, 1991.

Maggio, Rosalie, *The Nonsexist Word Finder: A Dictionary of Gender-Free Usage*, Beacon Press, Boston, Mass., 1988.

Mills, Jane, *Womanwords*, Virago Press, London, 1991.

Mort, Simon (ed.), *Longman Guardian New Words*, Longman Group UK, 1986.

Noble, Vernon, *Speak Softly – Euphemisms and Such*, The Centre for Cultural Tradition and Language, University of Sheffield, 1982.

Oxford English Dictionary, The (2nd edition on compact disc), Oxford, 1992.

Rees, Nigel, *Best Behaviour*, Bloomsbury Publishing, London, 1992.

Rees, Nigel, *Dictionary of Phrase & Allusion*,
Bloomsbury Publishing, London, 1991.

Rees, Nigel, *Dictionary of Popular Phrases*,
Bloomsbury Publishing, London, 1990.

Rees, Nigel, *Sayings of the Century*, George Allen & Unwin,
London, 1984.

Rees, Nigel, *Why Do We Say . . .?*, Blandford Press, London, 1987.

Tulloch, Sarah (comp.), *The Oxford Dictionary of New Words*, OUP,
Oxford, 1991.

The following newspapers and magazines have provided citations
and information:

*The Aberdeen Press & Journal, American Speech, The Author, Black
Panther, Black World, The Cape Times, The Christian Science
Monitor, The Courier-Mail* (Brisbane), *The Daily Mail, The Daily
Mirror, The Daily Telegraph, The Economist, The Evening Standard*
(London), *The Financial Times, The Globe and Mail* (Toronto), *Good
Housekeeping, The Guardian, The Independent, The Independent on
Sunday, The International Herald Tribune, The Lancet, The Library
Association Record, The Listener, The Liverpool Echo, The Los
Angeles Times, National Geographic, The New Statesman, News-
week, The New York Times, The Observer, Private Eye, Publishers
Weekly, Punch, Science News, Spare Rib, The Sun* (London), *The
Times, The Times Literary Supplement, The Sunday Telegraph, The
Sunday Times, Time, Tribune, The Washington Post, Video Today.*